Mental Habits

10 Lessons to Avoid Mind Traps, Rewire Yourself, Think Clearly, and Make Right Decisions

META CHANGE, MEGA RESULTS

ANDREW JAMES

Your Free Action Guide

Thank you for buying Mental Habits. A free **Action Guide**, workbook cum journal containing exercises to accompany this book is available for download. This is for helping you derive the most benefit out of Mental Habits. Type the following link in your web browser:

https://app.convertkit.com/forms/designers/1749784/edit

If you have any difficulty in downloading the Action Guide, contact me at:

andrewujames@gmail.com

CONTENTS

Stereotypes and The Law of Small Numbers ... 138

Memories Are Not Forever ... 152

Why Meta Mental Habits?

Did you ever fail at something? All of us do, sometime or the other. Be it big or small.

But you wonder: you thought about it, weighed the pros and cons, and made a decision. You took action. You were quick. And you were positive, full of vigor and passion. Yet things did not turn out the way you wanted.

Well, I too have failed a number of times—in small as well as big things. And I have met with success, too. Though a number of decisions were minor and reversible during the course of daily life, some were critical and irreversible.

At times, even bad decisions led to good outcomes, and to my utter surprise good decisions led to bad outcomes. Oblivious of my decision making process, I justified my successes to my skill, hard work, and positive attitude, while failures to coincidences and luck.

I have served in the Air Force, indulged in adventure sports, led million dollar negotiations, crafted strategy for organizations, even survived a killer earthquake. As part of high performance teams, I have worked under tight deadlines in uncertain, ambiguous, and risky situations. Sometimes, I could find reasons for not achieving the desired results in professional life. But I could also not ignore that in my personal life, like buying a house, a car, investing money, where to live, where to work and where to holiday, I could have made better decisions. I have made several flawed decisions, except for my marriage.

Well-meaning friends, self-help books, personal development gurus, and specialists in various fields were not of much use. They could not go beyond platitudes such as don't give up, be at it, be positive. Take action and you are certain to achieve your goal. But, I knew the failures were not due to lack of motivation or hard work or perseverance. Nor were they because of attitude or lack of action.

To tell the truth, just do it may be the worst strategy of all. We forget that before we act, we need to decide and decide correctly. And before we decide, we need to think and think clearly. This determines the inputs we use for decisions. Whether you are a formula one racer or a fighter pilot, a chess grandmaster or a basketball ace, a doctor or a soldier, a lawyer or a fashion model, an accountant or an investor, a CEO or a manager, the President of your country or a Professor, a marketer or a manufacturer, a knowledge worker or a manual labour, a chef or a designer—you need to think, either slow or fast. You may have a split second or a day at your disposal. But you need to think.

Quick action with any amount of hard work is no substitute for right thinking and decision making. Absent this, it's the classic case of rowing the boat with double the effort in the wrong direction. It took me years to realise there was a larger pattern at play in my failures and successes, all related to my thinking habits.

The easiest thing to do is to avoid thinking. The most difficult thing to do is to think clearly. Because thinking is hard work, it exerts a toll. Your primate brain is not of much help. Your mind fools yourself into taking shortcuts, and it creates mental traps. You stumble into these pitfalls and commit errors. More so with reversible and seemingly inconsequential decisions, you take decisions without really giving much thought. You jump to conclusions, going by instinct, believing you are following your intuition.

Your intuition, intelligence, and confidence are not of much use in thinking and deciding in a complex situation. In fact, at the time of decision, it's already late. You repeat shortcuts mindlessly, without being aware of them, and over time it becomes a habit. Without awareness, you remain in the vice like grip of your bad mental habits. These are the minefield of decision making.

Thinking clearly will also allow you to see how much to reflect, decide what to do and when to do. Those with a 'just do it' kind of mentality extoll the virtues of taking action as opposed to analysis by paralysis. Little do such people realise that being paralyzed and unable to act is itself an outcome of muddled thinking. **If you are thinking clearly, you will not wait forever to do something.**

Thinking precedes decision, which comes before action: **Think, decide, act**. Bad thinking leads to bad strategy, bad decisions and bad outcomes. Garbage in, garbage out (GIGO). Though the popular opinion would have us believe otherwise, mere doing cannot compensate for flawed thinking or not thinking at all.

Good mental habits aid you in thinking clearly, avoiding mental pitfalls. They will assist you in following a specific set of steps, a process or a routine, before you fast forward your thinking, decide, and act quickly. These are the master habits or the meta habits—habits of a higher order that direct all other habits.

Meta mental habits steer mini or atomic habits

Let's say you are a 29-year old person. Lately, you have been feeling energy less and lethargic, a little overwhelmed by life and need to improve your health. You may end up in a doctor's office, or meet a nutritionist, a fitness trainer, or even a life coach. Your meta mental habits related to perception, emotion, memory, thinking, reasoning, and judgement will determine what you choose to do. Again, you may decide to hire a fitness trainer and follow a strict schedule of diet and exercise. What diet you follow—vegan, Paleo, Atkins, Ketogenic, Mediterranean and which exercise—weights, long distance running or sprint, Pilates, yoga, CrossFit—you choose to do is a series of decisions.

Until now you are in the realm of meta mental habits. You can't escape meta as it is overarching. Meta is about—what, when, why, and where. Before you ask, what about mini habits or atomic habits. Both meta and mini habits are not antagonistic. Nor do they substitute each other. Mini habits complement meta habits. But mini is about how. Mini is specific to a context. Meta is universally applicable. Meta habits steer mini habits at all times. Meta is strategy, and mini is tactics.

You may be lacking in certain habits and use the technique of mini habits to build them. But meta mental habits already exist. None of us are without these: whether good or bad or flawed. Since, these are habits, they are unconscious and automatic.

Stepping out of your house to walk only 100 meters before you run, or doing only one push up, or writing only 50 words everyday by starting small and being consistent is in the realm of mini habits. Don't get the sequence wrong by putting the cart before the horse.

Now that you know how critical are the mental habits in our life, you need to improve, refine, and polish them. You also need to break bad ones, and build new ones.

When you rewire yourself with new mental habits, you provide gem of an input to your mind, changing the meaning of GIGO. It is no longer, garbage-in-garbage-out but **Gem-in-Gem-Out(GIGO)**. These are the new smart mental habits.

When you bring meta change, you get mega results.

How to Develop Smart Mental Habits?

Dilemmas, doubts, and confusion in thinking and decision making have confronted mankind forever. Risk, uncertainty, and ambiguity have been our constant companions. Since time immemorial, sages, philosophers and, recently, psychologists have alerted us to the tendency of our mind to lead us astray, referring to illusions, cognitive biases or fallacies.

The answer is scattered across fields: neuroscience, biology, history, philosophy, religion, behavioral economics, probability, neurology, computer science, literature, and psychology to name a few.

Finding the answer across one field does not work, though the research on cognitive biases comes close. In any case, research full of jargon that cannot be applied in real world is of no use. This book synthesizes the insights gained from various fields, aiming to provide a practical solution to the problems faced by us in our daily lives. It will ask you to imagine situations to illustrate a point or the limitations of our mind.

Developing new mental habits takes time. There is no easy way out. It involves change that again goes against our natural human tendency.

How this book will help you?

The method is proven. None of us are aware of these habits of the mind. But those who could change their habits, first became aware of their bad habits. These differ from person to person. Occasionally, I do come across people who go through the entire material presented in the book and claim they do not suffer from any of the mental flaws mentioned in the book.

If you are one of those, you are super human, and you really do not need this book. For the lesser mortals, let me assure you, hundreds who have worked on their mental habits felt improvement in their thinking and quality of decision making. After rewiring your mind with these habits, you refine and polish them with practice.

As we progress along, you will become aware of the traps that are a barrier to clear thinking. Our default thinking habits appear to be hardwired to stumble us. To avoid falling into them, we will learn from others' experiences and follow an action plan.

Whenever you are trying to change a mental habit, you have to approach your thinking in a mindful manner, not mindless. Changing the mental habits is a conscious effort, each and every time.

This book is accompanied by a free Action Guide, available for downloading from the link at the beginning. Together they will help you in:

- Understand the common mental traps in various situations
- Identify your habitual mental pattern
- Provide action steps to stop the bad mental habits
- Replace the old thinking habits with new ones
- Think clearly
- Take better quality and right decisions

While forming any new habit, you need to overcome the resistance, be consistent, and not put yourself under pressure of arbitrary deadlines. Some of you may have heard of the 21/90 rule for forming new habits. The 21/90 rule is not cast in stone. It may take more than 21 days to build a new one or break an old one, and more than 90 days to make it a part of lifestyle. Meta changes in mental habits rewire your brain. And that does not happen in an instant.

The best part, however, is you don't have to disrupt your existing schedule to accommodate anything extra. Do your daily activities as usual.

You can follow this 5 pronged strategy for changing your mental habits:

1. **Be aware**: Be honest with yourself, while identifying your bad mental habits.

2. **Choose wisely**: Go through the whole book once. Pick up one or, at the most, two interrelated habits that need attention.

3. **Patience**: Look for opportunities in your daily life. There is no dearth of them. Practice every day, be consistent, and have patience. Do the exercises in the action guide. If you stick to it long enough, you will form new mental habits and reap the benefits.

4. **Resiliency**: Years of habits cannot be changed overnight, and you may slip into your old habitual pattern. Get back on track as soon as you can.

5. **Review**: At the end of each day and every week, take stock of things, analyze, and apply the learning.

By the time you reach the end of this book you will be aware of the pitfalls of your mind. By rewiring yourself, you will learn how to think clearly and not be goaded by your instinct, feelings and desires.

You do not have to do anything extraordinary for mastering your life and work. This book will teach you how

MENTAL HABITS

doing ordinary things every day without falling into your own mental traps will lead to mastery in your chosen field.

I promise you will get it right.

Well begun is half done.

1

Fooled by Yourself

"The first principle is that you must not fool yourself—and you are the easiest person to fool. So you have to be very careful about that".

Richard Feynman

The roulette of life

Imagine you are in a casino. You have cashed your chips, ready to play roulette. As you approach the nearest table, you read the placard: "$5 minimum inside bets, $5 minimum outside bets. $1,000 maximum outside, $100 maximum inside". You are thinking should you bet straight up on one number as it pays 35 to 1, the highest paying odds.

You also catch sight of a board, highlighting the previous five numbers where the ball had landed.

Previous Wins
2
23
33
29
12

MENTAL HABITS

You think quick on your feet and observe: your lucky number 14 does not feature. You remember how so many people who bet on number 17 have won staggering sums. A scene from the classic James Bond movie, Diamonds are Forever, flashes through your mind. Sean Connery as James Bond places consecutive five bets on the number 17, despite losing the first two times and wins three times in a row. Alas, 17 does not feature. You decide to be a contrarian by betting on unlucky 13, but you can't spot that too.

Maybe you should bet on a number either in black or red. But will the ball land again on any one of these previous five numbers? Just then the dealer announces no more bets.

You wander across to another roulette wheel and read the board.

Previous Wins
1
34
7
21
9

Alas, the numbers 14, 17 and 13 are missing. How easy the decision would have been, if one of them featured on the board. You would have had some reason to justify your action. Scribbling on the score sheet, you try to find a pattern. You note the five reds in a row. Isn't it that a black is due, going by the law of averages.

It's good that you didn't bet on the first roulette table. Or, wait a moment. Going by the history, maybe the wheel on this table spins only red; you shouldn't bet a black on it. And, except for one number, rest are odd.

Well, I can hear you protest. Playing roulette has nothing to do with real life, and in any case, you are not a gambling person. You do not gamble, even for entertainment.

Roulette is just a metaphor for life. If something has happened more often in the past in your life, is it likely to happen again. Are you spotting a pattern or is it just a coincidence? And do remember, real life is far more uncertain, complex, and ambiguous.

While you can walk away from a roulette table, you cannot walk away from life. The wheel of life does not stop spinning. You make numerous decisions everyday with limited time, information, and resources.

Multibagger for becoming a millionaire

Let us move ahead. Imagine, you get an IRS tax refund of $10,000, least expected by you. You feel it might be prudent to invest your refund amount in stock market. You come across the stock of Netflix. You are fascinated by the company and even subscribed to its services.

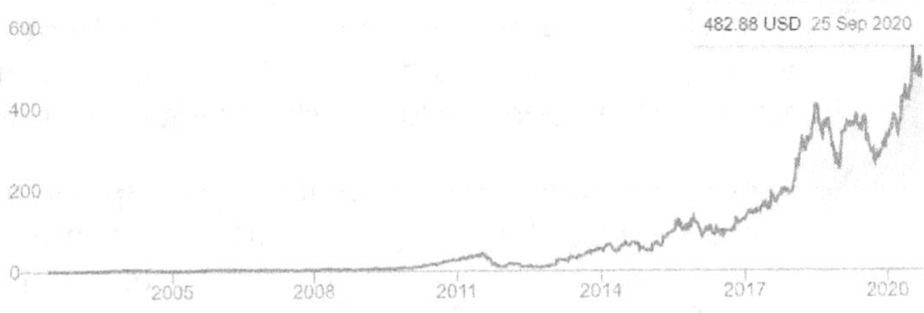

Price chart of Netflix (NASDAQ: NFLX)

The stock has been ascending since its listing in 2002, except for minor occasional lows, for a period of 18 years. Is it likely to climb further going by the past experience? Or is it long overdue for a fall? After all nothing goes up forever.

You are meticulous, methodical, and orderly. You did a little research on the internet. It reveals if you had bought one share during the IPO at $15, today you would be sitting on 3119% profit. A large number of analysts are predicting that the stock will reach a new high of $625 within 12 months.

The fundamentals of the company are sound. You have analyzed the stock the way a value investor like Warren Buffet would analyze. But Buffet himself doesn't invest in tech stocks. Your colleague at office, childhood friend, and a college pal who works in the bank are all urging you not to miss the chance.

You think past record of the company is enough proof that its share price will only go up. You can also hear the voice in your mind say what if the price tumbles. You may incur a loss. Anyway, it is found money, a bonanza due to tax refund. Hence, it's not worth thinking about so much.

Would you invest in Netflix stock or not?

The decision depends upon your thinking, understanding, and analysis of the situation. This in turn is influenced by your emotional state, instincts and perception.

More often than not, we take mental shortcuts, and our default habits hardwired into our brain with years of practice take over. This is where our mind fools us. Many of us believe we cannot be fooled by our mind. It's always the other people who deceive us, not we ourselves. If I have seen with my own eyes, then obviously it's true.

Can you trust your eyes?

See the image below. Do you see a young woman or an old woman?

You may see a young woman looking into the distance or an older unattractive woman looking towards the left. You can only see one at a time. If you can see only the young woman, then focus again on the picture until you see the old woman, and vice versa.

Here is a hint: the younger woman's necklace is the older woman's lips. The older woman's eyes are the younger woman's ear, and the younger woman's chin is the older woman's nose.

You may have come across this image before. You may wonder why we see a particular woman, old or young, first. A not so accurate explanation is our own age affects our mind's interpretation. Generally, young people see the attractive young woman, and the older people see the old woman.

That's beside the point for our purpose at hand. The main thing to note is that despite knowing the image represents both a young and old woman, our mind can see only one at a time. Therefore, in any situation there is always more to it than meets the eye.

What you focus on changes your perception and, hence, your perspective. The image never changes. What you see may not always be correct or the complete view of things. Personally, I always see the old woman first, and only when I focus my attention on other parts of the picture, the young lady emerges.

Consider the image below.

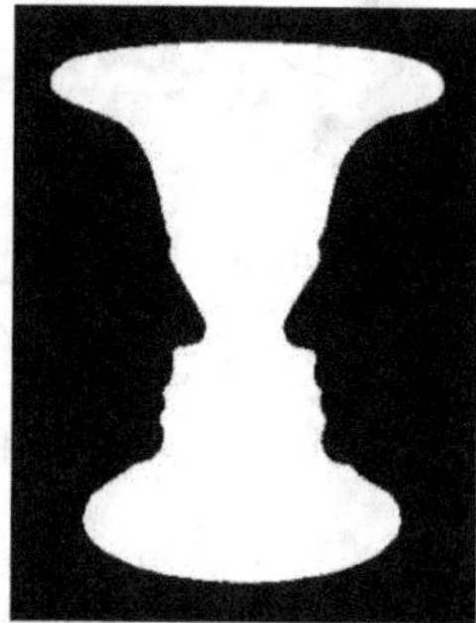

Do you see two faces or a vase? Which shape did you see first? Now see the other one. No matter how hard you try, you cannot see the first shape any more. You can see only one shape at a time.

When faced with ambiguity, our mind has severe limitations, influenced by memory and previous experiences. You only see facets of reality, not the complete reality at any given time. Therefore, it's useful to remember that our view of reality is always incomplete.

One-up on yourself

Our popular culture appreciates street smartness, celebrates winning, decimating competition by getting a leg up. What if you realize that before competing with others you need to compete with yourself? Before learning to be street smart in dealing with others, you need to become smart yourself. The street smart ones, the practical ones who are one-up on others have a smart mind, understand mental limitations better than most of us do.

You do not have to act smart with others, but you have to act smart with yourself, your mind. Meta changes in mental habits transform them into smart habits, giving you the edge. They help you avoid the mental traps, prevent others from taking advantage of you, and, most importantly, stop you from fooling yourself.

Quick Recap

- Amidst the uncertainty, ambiguity and complexity of life, we take mental short cuts in thinking and make decisions, without being aware.
- What you perceive with your own senses may be only the partial truth or slice of reality.
- To get ahead in life, we need not act smart with others. Acting smart with ourselves, by developing good mental habits to stop fooling ourselves is more important.

Rewiring

Complete the exercises in the Action Guide under Rewiring: 1. In the end, you should be aware of your broad decision making style in various situations.

2

Shatter Your Illusions

"For those in love with an illusion often refuse to accept reality."

Sanal Edamaruku

Different realities or illusions

Just as you are entitled to your opinions, so too you are entitled to your illusions, perceived as reality by you. An illusion is dangerous because you cannot distinguish it from reality. As long as you are under its spell, the illusion is the reality.

Take a bucket, and fill half of it with water. Put a stick inside the water. When you look at the stick from the side, it appears bent. You know it's an illusion as you can confirm it by feeling the stick with your hand. Or take the case of railway tracks that appear to narrow down, meeting far ahead, though they never do so.

You watch an animation, online video, or a movie. The brain perceives a series of images in rapid succession as a moving picture, known as phi phenomenon. Mere 24 frames or still images each second create the illusion of a motion picture. We accept these illusions and allow them to impact our lives just as reality would do.

Nature is not far behind in creating illusions. Due to Fata Morgana, mountain ranges in the polar regions appear distorted or stretched, and cliffs and coastlines though phantom appear visible. Mirages on land and desert appear like a body of water. These are not hallucinations as these occurrences can be captured by a camera.

Our illusions arise more often from our perceptions as we saw in the image about the young woman and the old lady in the previous chapter. What we perceive with our own eyes, we take it to be true. As we say, I saw it with my own eyes. But things get complex when all of us do not see the same bent stick inside the water. In most cases, each one of us sees a different reality as our illusions are different.

In February 2015, photograph of a dress posted on the internet went viral, with heated disagreements about the color of the dress. Some saw the dress as black and blue, others viewed it as white and gold. At one time 11,000 tweets using the hashtag, #TheDress, were tweeted per minute, leading to a total of 4.4 million tweets within 24 hours.

Does it really matter whether you see the dress as black and blue, or white and gold? Will resolving the mystery change our lives? You may dismiss it as much ado about nothing. It is no longer a trivial matter when you realise the processes underlying our perception of the dress are same as those determining our thoughts and perceptions about everything else in life, be it science, politics or culture.

Sometimes, it has to do with human biology. Look at the grid below in which squares are arranged in rows and columns.

When you look at the intersection of the rows and columns created by the squares, you see gray spots due to a phenomenon called lateral retinal inhibition. But when you focus your attention at any of the intersections, the gray spot disappears and looks white because we use different cells of the eye.

The tricky part is that even our knowing something is an illusion cannot ensure in breaking free from it. We do not see the world the way it is, though we believe otherwise: what we see of the world is the truth. Illusion is only a proof of this. It has to do less with your eyes and more to do with how your brain controls the entire visual system.

When somebody hits you on your head, you see stars in broad daylight. The impact on the head activates the neurons in the eyes, which the visual system controlled by the brain perceives as light though no light enters the eyes.

Usually, when faced with ambiguity, our brains fill the details with what we are familiar. Our earlier experiences, emotions, and presumptions shape our perception. Since these are different for each of us, our brains bend reality to match with inputs already available for reaching an inference.

In fact, as we progress along we will realize that we may suffer from multiple illusions.

Action tips: How to dispel illusion of reality?

Reality is all that exists whether we perceive it or not. The problem is we also perceive what does not exist, mistaking illusion for reality. This does not mean you will never trust your eyes again.

1. **Know you might be wrong**: Listen to different perspectives, and be open minded about your own. Your reality may be different from others or incomplete; hence, try to expand your view of reality.

2. **Cross check and question**: Verify, seek evidence, and question whether the person sitting across is an expert or a novice. Do it just like you would cross check a stick half-dipped inside the water is bent or not, by taking it out of the water.

Perils of overoptimism

Illusion of invulnerability

This arises from being an overoptimist. I know what you are thinking. What on earth could be wrong in being an optimist? Optimism helps in coping with stress and adversity, leads to better health, improves performance, and the list goes on. The benefits of optimism are proven. So far so good. The problem is those who use optimism as a crutch slowly slide into overoptimism and then into irrational optimism, when combined with other factors. Be positive at all times is the mantra reinforced by popular psychology, but then many are unrealistically optimistic, feeling invulnerable to all risk and danger.

A large number of us believe that we are unlikely to experience negative events as compared to others. The extreme optimists deep down in their heart feel that they are less likely than others to meet an accident, experience divorce, be laid-off from a job or fall sick. This is the "it will never happen to me" mind-set.

Perhaps teenagers put their belief in invulnerability to test more than others. Teens in California party a lot, a natural thing for most teens. However, a lot of teen parties were held in July 2020, when Covid 19 pandemic had already claimed thousands of lives. The incidence or death due to coronavirus amongst young healthy population is much lesser than the elderly. The younger lot who did not catch the virus or remained asymptomatic would always believe that nothing bad can happen to them, further reinforcing their sense of invincibility. In contrast, many middle aged persons who caught the virus could only express regret over their behavior before dying.

Pandemics are not everyday occurrences like hurricanes, floods, and earthquakes, and nobody expects to get caught in the midst of one. So we persist in our belief: not only misfortune is less likely to befall us, but also success is more likely to fall into our lap. A majority of us feel we will live longer than others, we will earn more than our peers, our children will do better than others, and our home will rise forever in value. But all of us cannot be better than everybody else or the average person. To put it another way, only a minority can be above average.

Such invulnerable people are also likely to drive drunk, not wear a seat belt, skip medical advice, and not contribute to their retirement savings because they believe they are less likely to meet with an accident, fall sick or run short of money in old age.

Notice the tendency to be overoptimistic and tilt the balance between optimism and reality far towards one side. A high degree of optimism does not prevent other cars hitting your car. As the belief increases that come what may good things will happen to you in life, you engage in risky behavior. Blind optimism is an illusion, more notable among youth.

Optimism is essential to human beings' survival and is encoded in our brain. But when you are blindly optimistic you tend to downplay dangers and ignore the cold brutal reality facing you.

Media and the popular culture, for instance, glorify the entrepreneur who despite all odds persists with his ventures. But most businesses fail. On average, in U.S alone 20 % of new businesses fail during the first two years of opening, 45% during the first five years, and 65% during the first ten years. Excessive optimism of entrepreneurs leading to strategic blindness is the primary reason startups fail. Entrepreneurs with moderate optimism set high yet realistic goals, whereas extreme optimists have unrealistic expectations and pursue too many opportunities. Realistic optimism may make you work hard and achieve your goals, but extreme optimism is delusional and leaves you disappointed.

Sometimes, overly risk behavior spurred by blind optimism achieves impressive results, but fluke is not sustainable over a long time. More often it results in unpleasant and tragic happenings. Overoptimism also leads to another illusion, that of planning.

Action tips: How to avoid illusion of invulnerability?

The root cause of feeling invulnerable is overoptimism and, as a consequence, highly risky, irrational behavior follows. This does not mean stop crossing the road or living life to the fulllest. Remember the following to avoid falling into this mind trap:

1. **Check your optimism levels**: Rational optimism accepts reality and is essential for well-being. Irrational optimism is what you need to guard against. Find a balance where you derive benefits of optimism and safeguard against unrealistic optimism. A glass half-full is better than half-empty. **Remember to have your glass half-full always, and no more than that.**

2. **Check your risk tolerance**: You may have high levels of risk tolerance, but it does not mean you should indulge in high-risk-seeking behavior.

3. **All risk cannot be known**: No matter what you do, all risk cannot be known in advance. What is unknown cannot be prepared for and catches us by surprise. Keep additional resources to tackle the unknown.

4. **Know the downside**: Understand the downside of your action, the impact it will have on you, including the ability to recover from it. If it is severe enough to make you insolvent, land you in prison or cause great harm to your reputation, do not act on it.

5. **Know the chances**: Remember that high-risk and low probability events like coronavirus pandemic, natural disasters, and road accidents do happen.

6. **No safety in numbers**: Your vulnerability or invulnerability does not depend upon a small or large number of people engaging in a particular behavior. A herd behavior does not make you invulnerable to risk.

7. **Do not succumb to Groupthink**: The tendency among the group members to agree on everything promotes a feeling among the group that the group is infallible. As a whole they cannot commit any errors of judgement. Do not have excessive belief in the abilities of any group as a whole, no matter how intelligent, skilled, and qualified are its members. Watch out for signs of ignoring danger, overoptimism, and brinkmanship.

Illusion of planning

Have you ever noticed a chronic tendency on your part to underestimate the time it takes to finish a task? And you do it despite knowing that you have taken much longer to finish similar tasks in the past. We all are too familiar with students overestimating their ability to submit term papers, class assignments, and theses, either in the nick of time or late. The same is true of your household chores, shifting your house, packing for a holiday trip as well as of constructing a new airport, bridge, or building. And all of us misjudge repeatedly, whether alone, or as a team.

Our judgement goes awry not only about the time, but also about the cost and risk. Research shows those who are meticulous finish their tasks well before the laggards do, but both types underestimate the time to complete a job. It appears impossible to learn from the past and plan accordingly. Despite knowing the past, we are doomed to repeat it.

Across continents and countries, cost overruns and delays plague projects. All these underestimate timelines and costs, and overestimate benefits. How pervasive is extreme optimism, and how pernicious are its effects in a group is nowhere more visible than in large infrastructure projects.

Sydney Opera House in Australia, now a World Heritage Site, with white-sail shaped shells on its roof is an iconic building with a breathtaking view of the harbor. However, equally incredible is the story of its construction turning it into a symbol of illusory planning as much as the destination of performing arts.

A renowned Danish architect Jørn Utzon was selected after an international competition in 1957. The construction commenced in March 1959 with an estimated cost of $7 million and was supposed to be completed in four years, opening on Australia day, 26 January 1963. The Opera House was formally opened on 20 October 1973, ten years later than the planned date with final cost being $102 million, the cost overrun around 1400%.

If you thought this was a one-off example of its kind, the list is endless and ranges from road and infrastructure to energy and sports events, spread across the world. Despite being aware that such projects often exceed either the budget or timeline, usually both, the executives in charge fall prey to planning fallacy.

As long as incurable overoptimists remain, time and cost overruns in mega projects will continue. Just as high school students continue to underestimate the time taken to work on their papers. And similar to your friend who does not wear a seat belt while driving feels he will never meet with an accident, and the person who smokes a pack a day feels he will never have cancer. Similarly, managers are always sanguine about their company than about the overall economy.

An old saying goes, 'If you want to make God laugh, make a plan,'. Or 'The best-laid plans of mice and men often go awry.' This does not mean we should not plan at all but plan without any illusions. The longer the planning horizon, the more our plans will go haywire as the intensity, scope and pace of change of modern life is fast, making our assumptions obsolete.

Action tips: How to ward off illusion of planning?

A lot of our time is spent on estimating various resources required to finish the tasks. You would have realized by now everybody is prone to planning fallacy and falls into this trap sometime or the other, underestimating time, costs, and risks. The eight most effective techniques for avoiding this mental pitfall when engaged in long and complex tasks are:

1. **Compare with previous tasks**: Compare your current task with a similar task you have performed in the past and recall the problems you encountered. Whether it is your personal project or any large-scale project, detach yourself and expand your view, accurately remembering the time it took. Analyze how this task is different from the previous ones and compensate for it by reworking your estimates downwards or upwards.

2. **Visualize scenarios**: After your initial estimate, go little deeper and take three more estimates: the best case, the worst case and most likely. For most of us, the best case estimate is same as the initial estimate. Worst case is when most of the things go wrong, and each step has a cascading effect. Likely scenario will be the past record with adjustments for the present situation.

3. **Take an average**: Let us say you are shifting your house from one corner of the country to another. You are

doing it for the first time, and you feel that it may take you anywhere between 10 to 15 days. Take an average of 10 and 15, i.e., 12.5 days, and round it off to 13 days.

4. **Base figure approach**: Take an initial estimate and add 20% extra resources as a buffer to arrive at a base figure and then fine tune it.

5. **Go granular**: For a task or project that is critical and irreversible, break it down into component steps, and calculate the time and cost required for it. Overlooking small steps that take time in the early stages of a project or taking them for granted may cost you dear as they will have a cascading impact. Check to be sure that the sum of the sub tasks does not exceed the initial estimate.

6. **Commit in weeks and months, not days**: The farther ahead in time is the deadline of your task and bigger the stakes involved, do not commit an exact date. Because life happens, and going ahead situations will come up that you cannot even imagine now. Let us say you are getting a fat advance for writing a book and you are keen to sign the deal. The publisher wants you to sign a contract for completing the book in 180 days, with a hefty penalty clause for any delay, not to mention the loss to your reputation. In such a case, make an initial estimate in weeks not days. If your initial estimate is 25 weeks, add a slack of one or two weeks, and sign the contract. When you commit in days, even if you are late by a day, which can happen, your plan goes for a toss, and you are legally liable. When you commit in weeks you have more leeway and less stress. Similarly, for a three-year, million-dollar project estimate and commit in months as far as possible.

7. **Beware of incentives:** Do not agree to an unrealistic deadline because the financial reward is too much to forego. You may justify to yourself that you can take a

chance, and you will figure it out as you go along. Go back to your best case and worst case estimates, and think about the quality of your work.

8. **Beware of social pressure**: Are you agreeing to an unrealistic deadline because you have a reputation of always delivering, no matter what happens, and you need to live up to that image in the eyes of peers, clients or your boss. Trying to look good can be costly.

9. **Do not confuse a plan with a goal**: Plan is only a means to achieve an end and should not become an end in itself. Be flexible.

****

The distortions in thinking, in memory and in judgement twist reality and are the fodder of overoptimism. Optimism is like a cup of coffee; a cup or two every day is all right. It gets you in the right mood, keeps you alert, and enhances performance. But 20 cups a day leave you anxious, irritable, and insomniac.

****

Illusion of learning and knowledge

Knowledge is power. Therefore, more the information, the better it is. You will judge events better. It will confer more power on you in controlling the events as the accuracy of your forecasts increases by possessing more information.

Unfortunately, it's not true. Knowledge is not power, but applied knowledge is power; unless information is used, it is of no value. Once you have loads of information, you cannot process all the information for making a decision but rely on a few key pieces, giving more weightage to a few than the others.

With more information, we chase information that is irrelevant, without knowing we are doing so. Or we lay too much store on information that is hard to find and have spent time and effort in searching.

Enough studies have proved that bookmakers in horse betting become increasingly confident in their prediction as the volume and variety of data given to them increases. The accuracy, however, remains the same despite the increase in data at their disposal.

In a slight variation, we also believe that we possess the knowledge available in the outside environment because of our indirect association. Searching the web creates the biggest illusion of knowledge. Three Yale psychologists carried out a study revealing that 'searching the internet for explanatory knowledge creates an illusion..., whereby people mistakenly think they have more knowledge "in the head", mistaking access to information for their own personal understanding of the information'.

Confusing freely accessible knowledge on the internet with knowledge in the head can have serious consequences. People inflate their self-knowledge even in unrelated domains, failing to monitor that internet was the source of their knowledge. The act of searching creates the illusion.

This has moved further ahead with abundant, free flow of information, especially on social media. Conflating what you read on a WhatsApp forward, or a Facebook post, or even a tweet, with your knowledge about the subject is far too common. This happens especially, if the information is presented in a fluent manner, deluding us into thinking that we have a good understanding of the subject and its underlying concepts.

When you read information multiple times because of the fluency of the material, you tend to equate your ability to recognize the information with your mastery of the material. You are still armed with little knowledge, which is dangerous.

We believe we know more than we actually know. It may happen that once we knew things. The fact that once we knew things only strengthens our illusion.

Perhaps, Daniel Boorstin summed it up the best: "The greatest obstacle to discovery is not ignorance—it is the illusion of knowledge".

Action tips: How not to succumb to illusion of knowledge?

1. **More is not better**: Avoid collecting more and more information in search of perfect information. Focus on collecting the critical pieces of information rather on volume of information.

2. **Don't swallow information**: Reduce the number of information sources to avoid information overload, and don't swallow information in large chunks without thinking. Be conscious of your inputs to the mind.

3. **Think and synthesize**: Relate the new information with your existing knowledge, and think of it as a whole. Draw your own logical conclusions.

4. **Prefer books**: Spend less time overloading your senses with T.V and internet. Instead read books to gain deeper insights as compared to videos and blog posts.

Illusion of control

People overestimate their ability to control events, even if the events are uncontrollable. If something they desired happens independent of their actions, they still believe that they were controlling it.

Have you noticed that those who get to choose their own lottery tickets feel they have a higher chance of winning compared to those who are assigned a random number. For winning the lottery you got to be lucky; therefore, choosing lucky numbers helps. Lucky numbers are chosen in myriad ways: based on birthdays, anniversaries, numerology, cultural or religious symbols, even shoe size.

Observe people while playing dice games like Craps in a casino. Players roll the dice very hard, if they want a higher number and very gently if they want a smaller one, thinking all along that they are in control of their fortune because of their skill. Children do the same while playing board games for fun. By any known law of physics, the speed of dice is not related to the number rolled. Those gambling with slot machines think they can control the outcome by pressing the handle in a particular manner. This does not stop here.

Remember the famous scene in the movie, Indecent Proposal. Robert Redford tells Demi Moore to roll the dice on his behalf and throw a 7 or 11. She kisses the dice and rolls it, landing a perfect 7, winning the bet. The person still gains control by transferring the responsibility to a luckier one.

As a positive illusion, the illusion of control helps in maintaining and enhancing self-esteem. People are more likely to fall into the trap when they are personally involved in a familiar task and gain some early successes in the chosen task with a large number of choices, alongside huge amount of information. The element of skill involved adds to the illusion. The more the competitive element, the grander the illusion.

MENTAL HABITS

The illusory sense of control on the one hand can make us persist in pursuing challenging endeavors, on the other hand it can induce us to take unnecessary risks. Financial traders indulge in excess trading, leading to decreased returns. A large number do not diversify their portfolio enough.

Humans since ages want to control the future by reducing uncertainty. In an uncertain situation, taking an unrelated action reduces our anxiety, bestowing a sense of control. In many cultures, tribals sacrificed humans to appease the Gods, thereby getting a control over their destiny.

Tennis champion, Rafal Nadal arranges his two water bottles in the same way. Tiger Woods wears a red tee-shirt on the final round of every golf tournament. Famous cricketer Steve Waugh used to carry his grandfather's red handkerchief in his pocket.

These are different from a pre match ritual to slowly get into the zone or flow. The superstitions and talismans provide a sense of agency. The tendency is alike in rats, pigeons, and monkeys. Humans are one of the oldest members of the club.

More than 50 years ago, a Harvard psychologist, B F Skinner, experimented with pigeons. Hungry pigeons were placed in a cage, and food was delivered to them through an automatic mechanism. Whatever actions pigeons were doing at the time of supply of food, they associated these actions with the food supply and continued with those actions. One bird, for instance, continued to turn anti-clockwise, another thrust its head in a particular corner of the cage, and two continued with a pendulum motion of the body. The pigeons too like many of the elite sportsmen exhibited superstitions, believing they were controlling the food supply with their specific behavior.

Hungry rats placed in a box containing a lever do something similar. As they move around, accidentally changing the lever's position, a pellet of food drops into a container next to the lever. Soon enough the rats push the lever to get the food, though the food would still come, if they did something else.

Continuing to guide the ball by twisting your arm long after it has left your hand and rolling down the bowling alley is no different. The illusion of control can be dangerous as people can accept blame for activities they do not control. Perfectionists tend to suffer more from this illusion. Some dwell on a past event, wallowing in regret, believing they could have changed the outcome of an event, only if they had acted otherwise.

In society at large, strong leaders project an image of being in control of things, and people who feel powerless in their lives often follow such leaders, giving up their free choices.

Illusion of control does have an unintended positive effect at times, when under the illusion we act with confidence and do not give up easily in case of failure. This is the attitude characterized in the poem Invictus: 'I am the master of my fate: I am the captain of my soul.'

Even those who discount lucky numbers and superstitions, succumb to the illusion of control because of the earlier two illusions, one of planning and other of knowledge. If meticulous planning and owning of knowledge does not give a feeling of control, then what else will.

Action tips: How not to falter under illusion of control?

Illusion of control motivates our behavior most of which may be harmless but not always. Finding the right balance of control is the key, without swinging the pendulum on the extreme from underconfidence to overconfidence. This is best summed up by the serenity prayer: "Grant me the serenity to accept the things I cannot change, the courage to change the things I can, and wisdom to know the difference."

1. **Know blind luck**: Understand you cannot control an event dependent purely on blind luck, for example, lottery.

2. **Know what you can control**: Understand the level of control you have by analyzing each element of an event and identifying the random events that can affect the overall outcome.

3. **Know how much you can control**: Understand to what extent events can be influenced by your skill and effort. Your circle of influence will likely be higher than your circle of control. Concentrate your energy accordingly. Don't be too hard on yourself.

4. **Don't feel powerless every time**: Take charge of situations which you can influence and control, for instance, your own health, changing a bad habit, battling an addiction or even bringing change in your personal life, family, community organisation, and society.

****

In the longer run, illusions seldom have a positive effect. When they shatter, the whole edifice crumbles along. Often illusions combine, the one of knowledge, when you feel you know more than others, and illusion of control, when you are certain you can influence the events of your life. The person under illusion almost inhabits an alternative reality. This cocktail of illusions can be heady, leading to overoptimism.

SHATTER YOUR ILLUSIONS

Illusions deceive us because we never know what conjures them. A series of them could combine to form a grand illusion. Magicians conjure illusions to amuse audiences, showing the difference between perception and reality. But we are prisoners of our illusions, created by our mind, mixing perception and reality, judgement and memory.

Change in this mental habit brings meta change in all other aspects of life. When reality hits hard, illusion shatters. Don't wait for that. Instead, shatter your illusions, if you want to build on your dreams.

****

Quick Recap

Illusion of reality

- We do not see the world as it is. We see reality as per our perception depending upon our earlier experiences, emotions, and presumptions.

Illusion of invulnerability

- Arising out of overoptimism, we believe we are impervious to all risks, negative events, and bad things will happen to other people, not us.

Illusion of planning

- In personal or professional life, when engaged in long and complex tasks, we go by best case scenarios, underestimating time, costs, and risks.

Illusion of knowledge

- Information collected from diverse sources, difficult to obtain, high volume or even the sheer act of searching makes us feel we are better placed to take decisions.

Illusion of control

- We overestimate our ability to control events and get a sense of control in an uncertain situation by taking an unrelated action.

Rewiring

45

Complete the exercises in the action guide under Rewiring: 2. You should be aware of the kind of illusions you are living under and start taking action to break their grip over you.

3

Ignorance is Confidence

"What gets us into trouble is not what we don't know; it's what we know for sure that just ain't so".

Mark Twain

High cost of overconfidence

The Costa Concordia, an Italian luxury cruise ship 290 metres long, carrying around 4,000 passengers sank off the coast of Italy on the night of 13 January 2012. It was bigger, technically superior and more luxurious than the Titanic, with four swimming pools, a casino, and a large spa. Fine weather and calm sea prevailed, yet it met the same fate as the Titanic.

Francesco Schettino, the captain of the ship, had been there, done that, seen it all before as far as sailing was concerned. He ordered the ship's state of the art navigation system turned off as he knew the area well and wanted it to be steered close to the island of Giglio for a maritime "salute", a common practice which Concordia had done in the past. The ship came too close to the shore and hit the rocks. Francesco was found guilty of manslaughter, causing a maritime accident and sentenced to 16 years in prison.

Like other human follies overconfidence too is universal, though tempered by culture and context. As we saw in the previous chapter, so many illusions can combine to lead us to a grand illusion of overconfidence—the certainty you feel in your own ability, performance, and level of control over various events.

Overconfidence is the most dangerous mind trap ensnaring humans, across fields: business, sports, finance, politics, military, academia to name a few. It is more rampant then we can imagine. The number of law suits filed by various parties who are overconfident of winning the case is astounding. No less is the number of wars started by countries who feel their military is superior to their neighbors or other nations.

The list of traders in the stock market who were sure of their skills in beating the market and brought ruin upon themselves as well others is huge. The number of those who feel they are excellent drivers is large. All of these are victims of overconfidence.

History is full of examples where overconfidence mixed with hubris prevents powerful leaders from changing their course. Napoleon's invasion of Russia claimed lives of 380,000 soldiers of the Grande Armée; Mao's Great Leap Forward contributed to the deadliest man-made famine starving tens of millions. British prime minister Margaret Thatcher remarked: 'You turn, if you want to. The lady's not for turning.'

Francesco still had reasons to be overconfident as he had been sailing for 20 years. But most of us feel overconfident of ourselves in fields in which we have no experience and skill.

Everybody is better than average

I know you never overestimate your knowledge, skills, morals, social standing, or intellectual abilities. Compared to others, people believe they are better than they actually are. This is more likely when the tasks are simple, and individuals believe these can be accomplished easily. How about going through these set of questions and rating yourself against each of these.

1. Are you a better than average driver?
2. Are you more ethical than your fellow students or co-workers?
3. Are you better looking than your classmates/ co-workers/ peers?

Most of us who answer the above questions are certain they are above average, better than their peers, more ethical, more intelligent, more interesting, and more attractive. More than 90% of Americans think they are more skilful and less riskier drivers than others. More than 80% percent of students feel they will finish in the top half of their class. More than 70 % of the lawyers believe they will win their cases.

Prisoners consider themselves as average in law abidingness but better-than-average in kindness, morality, ethics and other social traits when compared with non-prisoners. The list goes on.

While comparing ourselves to others, we consider our own best effort and outcome but instances of average behavior in case of others. We recall more favorable information when evaluating ourselves in relation to others. In our eyes, others' average performance represents their best, whereas in our case we pick better-than-my-average. We may even pick our aspirational behaviour for comparison with other people's actual behaviour. We are also inclined to use the same yardstick to judge ourselves and the person who is close to us, believing their best behaviour shows their true ability.

We do define others by their best, but those are top performers, far and few, whom we accept to be better than us. For instance, we do remember athletes for their best record setting performances, authors for their prize-winning books, actors for their award-winning movies, and singers for their greatest hits.

A majority of us, more than 50%, cannot be above average by definition. Though we do know you do not rate yourself as high as Tiger Woods in golf or Roger Federer in tennis, you may rate yourself higher than you actually are. People who in reality are above average in their skill rate themselves even higher, almost suffering from God complex.

We saw in the earlier chapter that those who were overoptimistic thought of themselves as better-than-average compared to others. They overestimated their chances of good fortune by comparing general life events such as winning a lottery or dying with cancer. However, here the cause of overconfidence is the wrong inference drawn by them to be better-than-average in specific traits when compared to others.

Why ignorant are cocksure?

On January 6, 1995, in Pittsburgh, Pennsylvania, U.S, a 45-year old man walked into Fidelity Savings Bank in Brighton Heights and robbed it in broad daylight. Then the 5 feet 6 inches' tall man weighing 270 pounds together with his accomplice robbed another bank, Mellon Bank in Swissvale. He did not try to conceal his face by wearing a mask or made any attempt at disguise while boldly robbing both banks, looking directly into the CCTV cameras. The man's name was McArthur Wheeler.

Later when he was arrested, he was incredulous as he 'wore the juice' while committing robberies. It took some time for the equally baffled police to understand why Wheeler was so surprised on getting caught. He was aware that lemon juice is an ingredient in creating an invisible ink. He thought if he applied the juice to his face he would turn invisible as well. Since robbing a bank is a high stakes game, too be sure, he even clicked a photo from the polaroid camera after applying the juice, though it stung his eyes. The photo came out clear.

McArthur Wheeler was sentenced to prison for 24 years. Though he may be the world's most incompetent criminal, Wheeler is a legend. His exploits in the short lived career are a testimony to his idiocy. His story inspired two Cornell University psychologists David Dunning and Justin Kruger to study human behaviour. In 1999, they tested participants on humor, grammar and logic. Those who fell in the lowest quartile, 25 %, overestimated their abilities far above average. Participants falling into 12th percentile rated their skill to be in the 62nd percentile.

People who are incompetent think they are much better than they really are, and a large gap exists between their actual performance and their perception about their performance. This is so because those who are not good enough lack the skills to know that they are not good enough. Lacking self-awareness, the below average overestimate their performance much more than the better-than-average. On top of that they are not open to criticism and not interested in improving themselves. However, when they are trained, they can appreciate the difference, although they would have never trained on their own. This applies across fields ranging from fire safety to maths skills to medical knowledge among surgeons.

A mediocre doctor ignores various possibilities of treatment, just as an ordinary lawyer fails to take note of a winning legal argument. In their professional and personal lives, people fail to realize their full potential as they are not aware of the possibilities. They do not know what brilliant, intelligent or smart in their field means.

One often sees this phenomenon in popular T.V shows like American Idol where the contestants come for auditions. A large number of them seem blissfully unaware of their level of incompetence and are crestfallen when rejected. Have you noticed something similar when your friends tell a joke, and it falls flat. They feel offended and shocked when the gathering does not laugh. It is difficult for them to fathom how bad they are at telling jokes. By the way, in general, men exhibit a greater tendency to be overconfident than women.

Action tips: How to tame overconfidence?

Wishful thinkers, overconfident jerks, and normal people, all fall victim to overconfidence, be it for a moment or a long stretch of time. You can counter the effects by doing the following:

1. **Challenge your ideas**: Remember you are human, and, therefore, you are not mistake proof. Invite feedback from your peers, friends, and associates. If you are a boss, yes-men may please your ego but entertain devil's advocates as well. Critics may not always be right, but at least you get a different perspective.

2. **Beginner's mind**: If you are new to learning a skill or a topic, beware that beginner's luck may make you overconfident. Be open to learning, and research the subject so that you take an informed decision. Combine modesty with enthusiasm.

3. **Prepare**: In positions of authority, you have to be confident in critical situations, otherwise your followers will not place their trust in you. A president of a country leading it through a national crisis or an army general on the day of a decisive battle cannot but act confident. However, meticulous attention to details, weeks of hard work, scenario planning, and extensive weighing of pros and cons goes into preparing for such a day.

4. **Go slow**: Don't take quick and impulsive decisions as you will be more prone to errors due to overconfidence.

5. **Reflect**: Be honest with yourself and recognize your limits.

6. **Remain grounded**: Success and accomplishments feed into overconfidence and lead you to believe what you are doing is right. Stay humble, and accept that we all have some flaws.

7. **Unknown unknowns**: There are things we are neither aware of nor we understand. Be ready for surprises as you do not know what problems are lying in wait for you. Also, you may not be reaching your full potential as you are not aware of what is possible.

Hindsight is not wonderful

You have always predicted the events accurately. Well, not in all fields but in certain areas. You saw all the bubbles in the stock market, before others could spot one. You knew this particular stock would go down, and how you wish you should have sold it. You seem to be clairvoyant.

But it is not so. You do not have a crystal ball. Otherwise you would have been extremely rich, accomplished, and on top of things. Sorry for breaking your illusion. What is true is that hindsight is 20:20. You suffered a loss when you did not sell that stock, accompanied by a regret. Along with this you think that you saw it coming all along, though it was only one of the several possibilities which you thought about. Whichever one would have turned out to be true, you would have been convinced that you saw it coming, and only if you had acted upon it.

IGNORANCE IS CONFIDENCE

You know your friends who forecast the rain; the friendly neighbor who knew the outcome of the soccer or basketball match; and your cousin, who predicted Barrack Obama will win the 2008 presidential elections, and again predicted Donald Trump's 2016 win. He wasn't surprised when Hillary Clinton lost. Among the many I-told-you-so were astrologers and fortune tellers, when Prime Minister Modi in India won a landslide re-election victory in 2019.

Smart forecasters do it all the time. Astrologers, of course, are smart enough to rationalise at a later date by talking in ambiguous terms like Oracles of Delphi did in ancient Greece.

When we fall into the trap of hindsight, the earlier events take on a new meaning as you align them with the outcome. You look backwards and say 'I told you so', finding an explanation for the outcome. Your doubt, hunch about things not turning out the way as expected is different from your claim now that you knew how things will pan out. How gratifying it is to believe your judgement always turn out to be right and how others lack the foresight and vision you possess, though it is your distorted memories playing tricks.

The effect is more pronounced in negative outcomes, especially severe ones, mainly because we pay more attention to events with negative outcomes than positive outcomes. It is indeed surprising that after we receive latest information, we revise our previous beliefs, selectively recall information, create memories without being aware of it. For instance, the more experienced the doctor, the more he is likely to believe he knew-it-all-along. As a result, we do not accept mistakes, do not learn from our failures, and we repeat the same errors. We tend to become myopic, focusing our attention on a single cause to understand the past, omitting other reasonable ones.

Soon this mistaken 'I-knew-it-all-along' belief turns a person into a Mr or Ms Know all, adding to the overconfidence of predicting the outcomes of future events as well. When you believe you have exceptional foresight, your excessive confidence is likely to nudge you to take needless risks.

Since millennia, historians have described the outcome of numerous battles with the benefit of hindsight, oversimplifying the critical moments where the leaders made wrong choices. Decades or centuries later, the side which appears victorious is a foregone conclusion. Complex situations of the past are looked at as linear simple binary decision making events, leaving us wondering at the follies of the losers.

In 2019, $ 4.4 billion were paid in the United States of America alone, as medical malpractice pay-outs. Out of these pay-outs, around one-thirds, $ 1.4 billion were on account of misdiagnosis or failure to diagnose. Now, patients must be able to prove at least three elements for a favourable judgement in a medical malpractice lawsuit. One, existence of a doctor-patient relationship; two, negligence on part of the doctor, by not providing treatment in a reasonably skilful and competent manner; and three, doctor's negligence caused actual injury to the patient.

Therefore, in such cases, if the litigant is able to prove second and third aspects, that is, doctor's negligence and consequent harm to the patient, he wins the case. But a misdiagnosis in itself is not an evidence of negligence. The crucial aspect is establishing if the doctor acted competently, which involves judging what the doctor did and did not do in arriving at a diagnosis.

By and large, to win a medical malpractice suit based on diagnostic error, the patient must prove a key fact: would a doctor in a similar specialty, under similar circumstances, have misdiagnosed the patient's condition. Radiology cases involving diagnosing from X-ray films, PET scans, CT scans requires visual identification of certain features. A patient undergoes a chest CT scan, and the radiologist interprets the film as normal. A year later the patient again feels discomfort in his chest and again undergoes a CT scan. This time the radiologist identifies a large tumour. On biopsy the tumour turns out to be cancerous; despite treatment, the patient dies.

The patient's family slaps a medical malpractice suit on the first radiologist claiming had he diagnosed the tumour correctly the patient would have been alive. The second radiologist appearing in the court, while viewing the first scan, seeing the tumour missed by the first radiologist, declares it was visible in the earlier scan.

The defendant radiologist is often judged by experts who have full knowledge of the outcome of the future scans. Psychologists believe this is visual hindsight, but it costs the other party dear.

In general, partiality due to hindsight is always stronger for the defendants in courts of law, as they are held to a higher standard and thought of as being able to avert the negative outcome. Plaintiffs do face the brunt wherein due to the negative outcome, the jury perceives the events as riskier, concluding that the plaintiff should have applied greater caution. Either the plaintiff or the defendant would have an unfair advantage

Most of us are wiser after the event. Once we know the outcome of an aeroplane accident, we know what the crew should have done differently. Let us not forget, at the time of the accident the crew did not know the outcome, and they did their best as per the situation.

Action tips: How to counter hindsight?

The antidote to this is:

1. **Be honest**: Keep an honest tally of what you know and what you don't know. Don't convert hunches, guesses, and speculations into facts at a later date.

2. **Record and review:** Record, what you knew at that time, and what were the assumptions, hunches and feelings. And as a consequence what did you predict. Finally, what did you do. When you review at a later date, analysing the accuracy of the forecast, notice that you assumed wrongly, but the forecast turned out to be right. Or the inputs were riddled with errors, or maybe the process of predicting was wrong. Design and trust your process.

3. **Reflect, reinterpret, and analyse**: Did you assign a single cause to an outcome of a complex event, leaving aside a host of other plausible reasons? Analyze which factors made a difference and which did not. Analyze without emotional attachment.

4. **Accept your limitations**: Sometimes we do not have answers to everything, and we may not know why something happened even at a later date, let alone predicting it. None of us have a magic crystal ball. Every time, we cannot understand what is going on. Don't create an explanation to make you and others feel better.

Why intelligent are full of doubt?

If at the one end are those with illusory superiority, then at the other end are those who suffer from Impostor syndrome. Those who suffer from this are overwhelmed with the feeling that they are not as intelligent, smart, or creative as others perceive them. Therefore, they do not deserve their success.

They live in constant dread of being found out and exposed as a fraud. Their success is a fluke, and the achievements are just a matter of happenstance or due to some external event outside their control. Maybe it was due to luck or timing or contacts or charm or a combination of these factors. It is not that they are underconfident in certain situations or lack self-esteem because highly successful people suffer from this. A constant fear nags them that they will be caught anytime.

A common script runs through these people's minds. The ugly little voice in the head says:

- I cannot afford to fail. Else, everybody will find out I'm an impostor.
- I am a fake. I am a phony. I don't belong here.
- I don't deserve all the opportunities. I was lucky.
- I am not good enough. They made a mistake.
- It's no big deal. Anyone could have done that.
- I could have done more.

Just when a person should be basking in the glory of her achievement and feel on top of the world, the syndrome strikes. The person devalues her own achievement, plays down her skills, and wallows in anxiety. All of them deserve to be where they are because they have earned their position. But they feel the opposite, that everyone around them is more accomplished, smarter and deserving.

Actor Judie Foster said, after she won the Oscar for Best Actress for 'Accused' in 1988, "I thought it was a fluke". I thought everybody would find out, and they'd take the Oscar back. They'd come to my house, knocking on the door,

'Excuse me, we meant to give that to someone else. That was going to Meryl Streep.'"

After gaining admission at Ivy League universities, students compare themselves to their classmates, feel they are underprepared to attend the classes, and even question the grounds of their own admission. Since there has been a mistake, they do not belong to the campus. Doctors who pass out of medical school feel they have not learnt enough to be treating patients.

Not only those who are starting a new job feel there has been a mistake in their selection but also experienced executives and CEOs share the same feelings of inadequacy. Howard Schultz, CEO of Starbucks says this about CEOs: "Very few people, whether you've been in that job before or not, get into the seat and believe today that they are now qualified to be the CEO. They're not going to tell you that, but it's true."

It happens at work, personal relationships and social interactions. The phenomenon is equally spread between men and women, though going by anecdotal evidence high achieving women seem more prone to discounting their efforts. Sometimes the only reason for impostor feelings is that you do not see many people that look like you or share the same background or are amongst the first few from an underrepresented community, feeling like an outsider.

For instance, computer science is dominated by white males, and being in racial minority as an African woman may trigger these kind of feelings. This may be the case with a black female DJ or an investment banker. International students in American universities feel the same. You meet fewer people resembling you, fight ingrained prejudices against stereotype and get a feeling that you do not belong to this place.

If you are a high achiever and feel like an impostor, you may be in august company of Neil Armstrong, Michelle Obama, Serena Williams and Tom Hanks. It's a pattern of thinking and feeling, a bad habit. Even first-time American Presidents have felt they do not belong to the oval office. And please remember, the mistakes you have committed are not a reflection of your overall competence.

Action tips: How to handle impostor syndrome?

Struggling with accepting success, praise, and feelings of inadequacy is common. If you feel like a fake, put the following tips to use:

1. **Stop comparing**: In this big wide world, someone will always be better than you. Use others' excellence to motivate you. You need not be the best to succeed in any field. Rather, strive to be unique.

2. **Relax**: Trust others who have put you in this position know what they are doing. Moreover, you are not responsible for other people's expectation of you.

3. **Replace negative self-talk**: If you keep on repeating negative thoughts, they will soon become a self-fulfilling prophecy. Replace the negative script in your mind with a positive one. As soon as your inner voice puts across a negative thought, don't fight it but gently add a positive thought. Let us say you notice yourself saying, 'I know, I'm not that good.' Immediately, add an empowering thought, 'I'm good' before the negative thought overtakes you.

4. **Know you are not alone**: Most of the achievers feel like an impostor for some time, believing that others are

better than them, and they will be exposed as a fraud. You are not alone.

5. **Don't seek external validation**: Don't always look for external praise or validation. Look at your accomplishment, and pat yourself on the back. Shake off the burden of society, parents, and friends, and stop achieving just to please others. You are worthy of your accomplishments.

6. **Forget perfectionism**: You will never know all there is to know about a field, be it computer programming, or playing a guitar, or writing a book. You don't have to know everything. Perfect is always an ideal, which can never be achieved. Others who seem perfect are no more intelligent or competent than you are. Many of them are just winging it or figuring it out just like you.

7. **Share your feelings**: Talk to your trusted friends, parents, teachers, coach, or a mentor in whom you can confide. You will find that many of them have been in this position before, and these feelings of doubt once in a while are quite normal.

8. **Acknowledge it and continue**: Don't stop what you are doing, especially if you are trying something new or outside your comfort zone. You will be most vulnerable to such doubts in these times. Press ahead. Act as if you are confident.

9. **Don't discount yourself**: Do not downplay your skills or talent that come naturally to you. Remember you are offering value to the world. You can be gracious, humble, and polite without feeling unworthy of your accomplishments.

****

Whether you are intelligent or wise, competent or incompetent, it's easy to fool yourself. You can fall prey either to underconfidence or overconfidence as well as to impostor syndrome. In such cases, self-awareness can help you find the sweet spot between overconfidence and underconfidence, or accepting your own success.

****

Quick Recap

Overconfidence

- Regardless of our competency level, it is easy to fool ourselves and feel overconfident.
- Overconfidence is the false assessment of our talent, skills, judgement, or intellect, leading us to believe we're better than we actually are.

Hindsight Affinity

- We have a I-knew-it-all-along tendency, assuming that we knew the outcome of an event, after the outcome is known. Or being wiser after the event. This know-all attitude also contributes to overconfidence.

Impostor syndrome

- Our feelings of inadequacy, continuous self-doubt and fear of being exposed as a fraud despite evidence of talent, accomplishment and success, which we attribute to chance or error.

Rewiring

After completing the exercises in the action guide under Rewiring: 3, you should be aware of the habitual patterns leading you to act overconfident, underconfident, or with impostor like feelings. You will have noted specific steps to be taken by you in different contexts.

4

Searching the Odd, Ugly and Inconvenient

"Men believe that which they wish to be true". (Homines quod volunt credunt)

Julius Caesar

I know what I am looking for

CEO/You: It's so obvious. The evidence is staring at us in the face, confirming all along what I thought was right. Let's not waste time by analysing the non-essential. Keep the focus.

After all the strategy sessions can be never ending. At some point or the other, you got to put an end to it. And we have seen every piece of data before us. The way we are going, we can keep on discussing till the cows come home. Sounds familiar.

That CEO could be you at work or sorting out your life. Only that you are fooling yourself because you did see every piece of data, but did not consider it. You discarded it

63

outright. The evidence did not conform to your view; hence, you did not prefer it. It was as good as not seeing it.

This tendency to use old and new information or interpret any information that supports our view and reject anything contrary, though unintentional, causes irreparable harm. Psychologists refer to this mental habit as the confirmation bias. The most dangerous thing about this habit is that your existing opinion influences your manner of perceiving information, without being aware. The havoc wrought by throwing out disconfirming evidence while taking decisions can only be matched by its omni-presence. This is pervasive, pernicious, and the most denied mental habit. Rare would be a person, who accepts it.

Newspaper reporters and T.V. show hosts interview experts who support their prior opinion; researchers undertaking experiments gather information supporting their preconceived conclusions; employers who believe Ivy league graduates are highly intelligent pay attention only to this fact and ignore other information on the CV.

My best friend believes left-handed people are highly creative and talented. He cites guitarist Jimi Hendrix, artist Leonardo da Vinci, Michelangelo, Napoleon Bonaparte, President Barack Obama, Albert Einstein, Neil Armstrong, Bill Gates, Steve Jobs, Mark Zuckerberg, Oprah Winfrey, Beethoven, Charlie Chaplin among others in a long list. Adding sports persons like Rafael Nadal, Babe Ruth, Martina Navratilova, Ayrton Senna and Brain Lara, the list is impressive. But what about those who are left-handed and not creative?

Seeking confirming evidence

Each card has a number on one side and a patch of color on the other. Which card or cards must be turned over to test the idea that if a card shows an even number on one face, then its opposite face is red?

The most common answer is the card with number 8 and the one in red. This answer, however, is wrong. In this case, you chose the cards that confirm the statement rather than disconfirm it. The correct answer is the number 8 card and the brown card. An explanation of the right answer is in the annexure at the end of the book.

The causes for picking information vindicating our stand are as numerous as the contexts where we do so. Looming deadlines, data and information overload, physical and mental tiredness, all nudge us towards this mind trap. Racing against a deadline, last thing on our mind is to search for disconfirming evidence. Disconfirming information discomforts and slows us down. Small wonder, we ignore it, though unintentionally. Whereas, picking up a fact that has an immediate effect on the task at hand adds to the illusion of control. But running too fast on a road full of pit holes, we are likely to fall into one.

Many psychological studies suggest adults can hold only a limited number of separate pieces of information in their working memory: it varies from five to nine. Some even peg the number at four. Separating wheat from the chaff is important for your mind. It reduces complexity. But while winnowing do you blow away the grain, or the husk, or some grain along with husk. Our response to complexity is simplicity as it brings down the information overload. At the same time, reducing complexity by stripping off the critical information may produce lopsided simplicity with its own perils.

As we simplify the mental processes related to—perception, emotions, memory, thinking, judgment, and reasoning—for understanding reality, it also satisfies the human instinct for storytelling. A neat compelling narrative combining selected events brings coherence to an otherwise chaotic world, influencing the listeners. Meanwhile, retelling the same story deepens the narrator's beliefs. Stories by definition have some form of emotions into their making and, therefore, cannot be objective.

The tendency to confirm our prejudices also hurts our relationships. If you believe your partner does not care for you anymore, you will continually look for evidence that supports your belief. You will tend to ignore all the instances that might prove you wrong. One incident adds to the other, and after a few months you may be fully convinced that your observation about your partner was true.

If you have inferred that your co-worker or relative is nasty, you will begin to collect the evidence to prove your inference is true, ignoring the contradictory evidence. If you hear something negative about your best friend, you will dismiss it as a rumor. If you are convinced old uncle Jim is always crabby, cynical and senile, you will look for confirming evidence, ignoring the time he is happy, positive, and alert.

SEARCHING THE ODD, UGLY AND INCONVENIENT

Under the influence of our habit to prefer confirming evidence, despite seeing all the information, our perceptions distort it. That is why often we see two people agreeing on the same set of facts holding strong divergent opinions on a subject. You and I can see the same figures, numbers, facts and perceive it differently. More information or better quality of information is no solution.

In the words of stock market wizard and investor, Warren Buffett: "What the human being is best at doing is interpreting all new information so that their prior conclusions remain intact." In the stock market, investors search for techniques that align with their investment philosophies.

You often conclude that you have discerned a pattern. Whether it is searching, gathering, preferring and interpreting evidence, or recalling information, testing assumptions and framing a situation, you are confirming your beliefs. Picking your own bits supporting what you desire to be true is easy, but risky.

While leading a team, a leader may sway the team's decision to his liking by his sheer eloquence, past reputation, all the while acting on his prejudices. An astute leader will find ways to elicit contradictory opinions and information, without letting the ego come in between. Too often, self-esteem and the desire to seem consistent prevents leaders from accepting a different view point.

Unaware and without any intention to selectively seek and interpret evidence, people engage in one-sided case building like lawyers and debaters who do it deliberately.

Astrologers, fortune tellers and mind readers benefit by people's propensity to give more weightage to confirming evidence than to disconfirming evidence. A mind reader describes personality and character in generalised and universal terms. A person who believes his mind is being read can easily find evidence that fits in with this belief, ignoring what does not fit in. Seeing what they are looking for, believers in astrology easily find examples of predictions turning out to be true, forgetting the prophecies that did not materialise.

In every field, from sports to movies, business to fiction writers, tens and thousands of people fail. But media captures only the success stories that are far and few. The failed are forgotten.

Cicero recounted a story about the atheist Diagoras, who was shown a painting of those whose prayers saved them from a shipwreck.

"See," says he, "you who deny a providence, how many have been saved by their prayers to the Gods."

"Ay," says Diagoras, "I see those who were saved, but where are those painted who were shipwrecked?"

We focus on those who survive, not on those who perish.

Witch hunting

The pitfall of the mind to confirm our beliefs has been with us since time memorial. Nearly 2500 years ago, the Greek historian Thucydides remarked, 'it is a habit of mankind to entrust to careless hope what they long for, and to use sovereign reason to thrust aside what they do not fancy'.

In medieval Europe, a woman who was accused of being a witch often had to undergo a test, a trial by ordeal to prove her innocence. One of the infamous tests was the cold water test: accused witches were dragged to the nearest body of water and thrown into it. If they floated, it was proof of their being a witch, and they would be burned or hanged to death. If they did not float, they would be considered innocent, but they would have died anyway.

SEARCHING THE ODD, UGLY AND INCONVENIENT

People's belief in witchcraft was strong, and special rules of evidence were applied in such trials. Bodinus, a 17th-century French authority on the subject stated: 'The trial of this offense must not be conducted like other crimes. Whoever adheres to the ordinary course of justice perverts the spirit of the law, both divine and human. He who is accused of sorcery should never be acquitted,.... for it is so difficult to bring full proof of this secret crime, that out of a million witches not one would be convicted if the usual course were followed".

We do a similar thing with information, opinion, or evidence we do not like; we evaluate disconfirming evidence with a bias and kill it.

Those in support of gun control in the U.S. will cull out news, stories, and opinions that curb gun ownership. On the opposite spectrum, those opposed to gun control will line up information consistent with their view. Even the news of any mass shootings will be interpreted to support their beliefs.

We remain loyal to certain brands as we develop a positive bias toward a particular product and view all information favourably. Once we develop a bias for BMW, we will view all data related to BMW cars in a positive light than, say, Audi cars. In fact, car owners who are loyal to a particular brand end up paying more for the new car when replacing the older model with the same brand. Those who prefer a specific brand are less likely to negotiate and bargain hard.

Doctors who have already framed a hypothesis about a patient's disease are likely to misdiagnose, as they tend to overlook the disconfirming evidence. They only look for evidence that confirms their preliminary diagnosis. For that matter, hypochondriacs look for evidence to prove they are suffering from a particular disease.

Filter bubble

When you are living in a filter bubble, you receive skewed information or you choose to receive information only from specific sources. Social media companies already cater to this requirement of subscribers, by allowing to curate feeds. Facebook's newsfeed is one example. The algorithm decides what a user would prefer to see based on location, past behaviour, and search history. Getting news from a WhatsApp group is another.

In today's world, politics is an area where people are highly opinionated, and emotions come into play. Everybody and their uncle have an opinion. The debates, discussions are polarised as the evidence is cherry picked by ideologues and adherents of both sides, widening the divide. Be it democrats versus republicans in the U.S., labour versus conservatives in the U.K, or the right versus the left in India. Users do not wish to interact with those holding opposing views, and the posts they see are in line with their views, reinforcing their beliefs. Filter bubbles reinforce our beliefs.

5 Steps to fall into confirmation trap

It's easy to fall into this bad mental habit. The five missteps are:

1. Form an opinion.

2. Find data, evidence, and pattern in support of your opinion.

3. Select facts that your target audience will find convincing. Repackage and refine evidence for a neat fit with your opinion.

4. Add emotion, and turn your opinion into belief because you are right.

5. Ignore, discount, and discredit all new information so you don't have to revise your belief.

Action tips: How to overcome the impulse to confirm our beliefs?

No matter how hard we try to be objective, some bias will always shape our opinion. This natural tendency grows stronger when the information is ambiguous. Mere knowing this fact or wanting not to fall into this trap is not enough. You need a practical method to do so. A few ways to overcome this are:

1. **Take your time and explore**: Before making a decision, take your time in finding out more about a subject, talk to the people, and explore with an open mind. Don't immediately stop gathering information, if you notice a pattern. In the end, you may weaken your first impression, if not change your opinion.

2. **Search for the opposite**: Form alternate hypothesis; in fact, time permitting form at least two or three, if not multiple choice of actions. Actively search for disconfirming evidence contrary to your initial views, and be willing to change your opinion.

3. **Argue for the opposite side**: When in doubt adopt an opposite viewpoint for the sake of argument, marshalling facts in support of opposite viewpoint, to the point of proving yourself wrong.

4. **See your relationships with new eyes**: Admit you may be under the influence of this bias. View your interactions with people with a fresh pair of eyes, keeping an open mind, looking for proof contradicting your opinion. For example, in relation to somebody

whom you consider selfish, look for times when they are considerate.

5. **All data is equal**: Give equal weightage to all data, do separate good data from bad data, distinguish fact from opinion, and identify isolated facts from facts in context. Avoid temptation to filter data. When seeing a portion of data, it is easier to align it for supporting a belief rather than refuting the belief.

6. **Neither love nor hate drive you**: Are you already in love with a particular decision, or you hate a particular course of action? When you love something you will tend to overstate its benefits, but when you hate something you will highlight its drawbacks. Are you downplaying the risks or amplifying rewards?

7. **Observe your reactions**: Take note of the type of information you agree with readily. Also notice your reaction to information with which you agree as well as disagree. Observe what you pay attention to and which information you choose to ignore.

8. **Focus on decision**: Keep the focus on the decision you are trying to take and not get lost in the jungle of opinions. Eliciting opinions is only the path towards arriving at a decision.

9. **Change the order of accessing information**: Plan and be clear about the decision making, especially, the criteria for decision making, before you start searching for information. Do not change the parameters for decision making after you receive information. Let us say you enter a store to buy a shirt under $35. You notice a shirt that you like, but the price tag is $55. You change the goal post by justifying to yourself how this shirt is worth $55 and meets your requirement.

10. **Check your ego**: Are you in a position of authority or leadership, and you fear that if you change your opinion, your followers are likely to view you as vacillating, fickle minded, and weakling. Don't be rigid about appearing steadfast, clearheaded, and firm at all times. Your ego succumbs to the pressure to seem consistent.

****

When under the grip of this mental habit your motto is: First I believe, then I see what I want to see, and I hear what I want to hear. The unfortunate part is that you are not aware of it.

Since, we believe we have reached our conclusions through reason and evidence, we justify our beliefs and actions to ourselves and others. We embrace information that suits prior beliefs. None of us like to search for the odd, ugly, or inconvenient.

Quick Recap

- We have an inclination to search, interpret, recall old or new information that supports what we believe to be true, subconsciously ignoring what is otherwise.

- Rather than see and then believe, under the influence of confirmation bias, we first believe, and then see to suit our beliefs.

- We respond to complexity by picking evidence selectively, simplifying things for quick processing and falling into this mind trap.

Rewiring

Complete the exercises in the Action Guide under Rewiring: 4. In the end, you should know how and when do you selectively pick information to suit your beliefs along with reasons for doing so. Make your own action plan as per the 10 Action Tips above.

5

I like to win, but even more, I hate to lose

"Our doubts are traitors, and make us lose the good we oft might win, by fearing to attempt". - William Shakespeare

A weird loss and crazy hope

The Barings Bank founded in 1762 was the United Kingdom's most distinguished financial institutions and the world's second oldest merchant bank. As a part of its illustrious history, the bank had funded the construction of the Panama Canal and the purchase of Louisiana from France by the United States of America. It even counted the Queen as one of its customers.

In February 1995, the then 233-year old bank collapsed overnight. ING bought it for £1.

Nicholas William Leeson, a young Englishman aged 25, had joined the bank in 1989 as a trader. In 1992, Barings opened a Future and Options office in Singapore for transacting in the Singapore International Monetary Exchange (SIMEX). Nick Leeson, or Nick as he was called, was appointed General Manager of the new office. Trading aggressively, he made large profits in derivatives trading. In 1992, his profits constituted almost 10% of Barings' total annual profits, earning him a bonus of £130,000 on his salary of £50,000. Within the bank, he commanded an aura of infallibility.

When Nick lost money in trading operations under his watch, he hid the losses amounting to £20,000 under an error account, hoping to recover them. The losses in this secret account kept on accumulating, reaching £2 million, soon touching £23 million at the end of 1993, swelling up to £208 million at the end of 1994, despite few recoveries in between.

One fateful day on 16 January 1995, he placed a short straddle on the Singapore and Tokyo stock exchanges, hoping that the market would not fluctuate much. However, in the early morning on 17 January 1995, an earthquake hit Kobe in Japan, and the Asian markets plunged.

He made further risky trades again in the hope Nikkei, the Japanese stock index, would recover. His hopes were dashed and the Barings' stared at a loss of £827 million or $1.4 billion, twice its available trading capital. The Barings bank went bankrupt, and it was no more.

Apart from the governance, the key factor that led Barings to perish was the human psychology, the propensity to avoid losses. A loss isn't a loss until I take it. This is how so many investors rationalize their fear of loss and hold on to losing investments. To avoid experiencing the pain of real loss, they will hold on to a losing investment much longer than necessary and end up suffering much bigger losses, just as Nick Leeson did.

Investors hold stocks that go down in price and sell those that have risen in price. Riding losers in the belief that they will bounce back and cutting winners is the default mode. Of course, by avoiding to sell the stock at a loss, they avoid accepting that they made a judgement error, their pride coming in the way. But biting the bullet is not easy. Some sell stocks as soon as they rise in price just to lock in the profits, goaded by both fear and pride.

A bird in hand is worth two in the bush

Humans dislike losses and prefer gains. This is no earth shattering piece of wisdom. Even our close cousins chimpanzees prefer gains to losses. But it could be a eureka moment, if you will note that humans dislike losses more than they like gains. Even if the odds are same, we will prefer not to lose $500 than gain $500. In fact, Capuchin monkeys when trained in a study showed the tendency to avoid perceived losses just like wall street traders. This shows that our ancestors and us may be hardwired by evolution towards loss aversion.

Moreover, losses hurt us much more than equivalent gains. Consider the following gamble:

- 50 percent chance of winning $150
- 50 percent chance of losing $100

People do not find the above proposition appealing, as loss of $100 imposes far greater psychological costs than the gain of $150. The minimum gain that people need for the gamble to be attractive ranges around from $200 to $250. In other words, people dislike losses two to two and a half times than they enjoy gains. Or by gaining something you will be half as happy as losing it you would be unhappy. Unless you win $200, you will not consider losing $100. Your behavior in the face of uncertainty is anything but rational.

The scenario may involve an outcome due to investing in stocks or a house. This response shows how negative emotions dominate us, leading us to focus on setbacks than on progress. A critical comment may impact us more than a praise. Probably, it would need more positive comments for us to offset a negative comment.

Pain of losing is more than the pleasure of gaining, even if the item has been in your possession recently. Ownership makes parting with an item emotionally painful.

Little wonder, we find it so difficult to declutter our homes. Suddenly you become overly possessive about something that you own but has not been used for quite some time. The shoes, CDs, clothes are the same as available in the market, but they turn into something special because as an owner, you assign more value to them. This sense of psychological ownership prevents you from discarding a lot of items you own. You invent all kinds of seemingly logical reasons for keeping the junk: something is useful; one has emotional value; and another looks expensive. While selling something, you price it higher than somebody would pay for it.

The moment we have a sense of ownership about a thing, our behavior to continue ownership is anything but rational. During auctions, people experience a premature sense of ownership and would do anything not to lose the item, even if it means they end up paying a high price by bidding higher in each round. When you test drive a car, you imagine what would it feel to own it. Even imagining ownership can increase the value you assign to something.

Now, think of the following three scenarios:

- A one in a thousand chance to win $1 million.
- A 90 percent chance to win $10 and a 10 percent chance to win nothing.
- A 90 percent chance to win $1 million and a 10 percent chance to win nothing.

A possibility exists of not winning anything at all in the three options, but the psychological impact would be different in each of the cases. In the first scenario, as such the chances of winning are not very high; in the second, amount at stake, $10 is too small; however; in the third scenario, the sum is large and the chances of winning are quite high. Anticipating gaining $1 million with a very high chance, most people would even start planning about spending the bonanza. The imagination would instill a sense of ownership. But when it doesn't turn out as anticipated, it would induce a big sense of loss, upsetting most people.

In situations where no risk exists, the value of an item increases for the owners, once they own it. Giving up the item is a kind of loss for the owners, and they feel it much more strongly than receiving it, a kind of gain. People are willing to pay much lower to acquire something than the least amount they are willing to accept to part with the same thing when they own it. This happens even when the item was obtained a few minutes ago.

In one classic experiment, participants were given a chocolate bar or a coffee mug for free, permanently. Many participants who were first given a chocolate bar were unwilling to exchange it for a coffee mug, and similarly those who were first given a coffee mug were unwilling to trade it for a chocolate bar. Mere ownership of an object changes its perceived value in our eyes as we get emotionally attached to it. What belongs to us seems more precious to us, when giving away.

Not only material goods but a sense of ownership of ideology in politics or in sports makes us value it much more than its worth. We feel a kind of investment in the opinions.

For the same reason, once you buy a high-end car or a luxury house, thinking you will move back to your previous standards, if need arises, does not work out. We adjust fast to any improvement in our lives. Scaling back your standard of living can be painful. Rich are often vulnerable to the anxiety induced by the thought of losing their wealth. The moment we gain influence, power or wealth, the new position is the normal against which we judge our future gains and losses.

You love risk when faced with losses

Psychiatrists label people who behave very differently at different times as having a split personality. The condition is also known as multiple personality disorder or dissociative identity disorder. It seems most of us do exhibit different personalities in various situations.

Related to our aversion to losses is another aversion, one related to risk. In face of risk, the choices we make when facing potential losses are different from those we make when facing potential gains. Take this choice between two lotteries:

- Get $900 for sure, or
- Have a 90 percent chance of getting $1,000.

Now consider this alternative set of choices:

- Lose $900 for sure, or
- Have a 90 percent chance of losing $1,000.

In the first set of choices, a risk-averse individual will choose the first option, and a risk-loving individual will choose the second. When faced with a risky choice leading to gains, generally, most people choose the first option, risk-averse as they are.

In the second choice set, however, most people choose the second option. In short, when facing potential losses, people become risk-seeking rather than risk-averse. Thus, people can be averse to risk as well as seek risk depending upon the situation.

Also, people evaluate an outcome related to loss or gain from a reference point, usually their current level of wealth, specific to each person. However, the reference points can be aspirational, what we are hoping to achieve, what we believe we deserve, and what we are striving to achieve. People may view anything below the reference level as a loss and may be willing to take risk to achieve gains.

No wonder, those who have lost money since afternoon, bet heavily on the last horse race in the evening, willing to risk losing more money in the hope of making good their earlier losses. We don't even know we love risk when faced with losses.

How casinos make you lose money?

As the old joke goes, a guaranteed method to go into a casino and come out with a small fortune is to go in there with a large one. Casinos are designed to win in the longer run as the games are tilted in the house's favor. But the task for the casinos is not easy. Occasional wins to sustain the players interest in betting and also inducing players to continue playing and losing money is a tough balancing act.

They divert players' attention by offering free food and drinks, served by attractive waitresses, free stay in the hotel, taking care of basic needs. These small rewards offset the sense of loss, with patrons feeling they have got some of the money back. They mitigate the fear of loss as money changers convert the currency into chips, tickets, and coins, which does not evoke the same sense of financial loss as handing over cash does.

You lose track of time as well as the money you lose, staying longer and spending more than planned. Once you are faced with a loss, especially if you have gone beyond the limit you set for yourself, you will indulge in riskier behavior. Feeling guilty as your emotions take charge, you will take more irrational decisions.

Credit card companies have known all along our psychological comfort to pay for things by a credit card than in cash. The plastic card remains the same, but parting with cash makes us feel we have given something away.

World's deadliest air accident

The mentality of avoiding losses led to the deadliest air accident, causing biggest loss of human lives in aviation history. In March 1977, a bomb exploded at a flower shop in Las Palmas Airport on the Canary Islands. As a result, a Boeing 747 KLM Flight 4805 that had left Amsterdam and bound for Las Palmas Airport was diverted to Tenerife Airport on the Spanish islands along with many other flights.

Captain Jacob Van Zanten of the KLM flight was one of the world's most experienced pilots, who also headed KLM's safety program and was a kind of celebrity in the pilot community.

The small Tenerife airport with a single runway was soon choc-a-bloc with many parked airplanes blocking the runway. In addition, the fog reduced visibility, delaying clearances for take-off. Around 1 p.m., Van Zanten calculated that if he did not take off in a few hours by 6.30 p.m., his mandated rest period would start. This would trigger a series of events: since no replacement crew was available, the flight would not be able to take off. And around 500 passengers would be stranded overnight. The KLM airline would not be able to find enough hotel rooms to accommodate them on this island. The delay in this flight in turn would lead to cancellation of other KLM flights.

Meanwhile, he decided to refuel at the island to save time when he later landed at Las Palmas. As he decided to refuel, word came that Las Palmas had reopened, but he could not stop the refueling in between. By the time he finished, heavy fog covered the runway, visibility reduced to only 300 meters. Van Zanen became edgy with potential losses plaguing his mind.

He decided to take-off asking his copilot to obtain ATC's permission as the plane moved forward. The copilot did receive clearance, but for the airway clearance, and not for the takeoff clearance. He continued, wrongly presuming ATC had permitted him, oblivious to a Pan Am airliner on the runway hidden in fog. Although he tried to avoid a collision by taking off early, the underbelly of the KLM plane hit the top of Pan Am aircraft, exploding into a ball of fire. The impact and the fire resulted in 583 deaths, killing the entire crew and passengers on board the KLM flight, along with many Pam Am passengers.

The enquiry revealed the mental state of loss aversion was a factor in the KLM flight accident. The losses that played on the captain's mind included a lesser mandated rest period due to the flight delay; cost of making the passengers stay at the hotel; and a mark on the pilot's reputation of being punctual. A combination of these affected the decision making skill of an experienced captain. The greater the importance we attach to the potential loss, the more we behave in a risk averse or risk seeking manner.

Starting a war to avoid loss

Clashes, conflicts, and wars may happen because each side believes it is defending the status quo, that is, it will incur large losses if it does not fight. With perceptions, stereotypes, and weight of history behind them, both the sides overestimate the other side's hostile intention. The other party is perceived as making every effort to gain at their expense and not willing to back down. The only option is to take strong and aggressive action to avoid losses. History is full of such examples where countries have been pushed into wars to avoid losses than to make gains, fear and insecurity being the prodding factors.

How we spend money to avoid loss?

Since decades marketers have been triggering a fear of losing out on a great offer, nudging us to buy. A common technique involves all or some of the steps:

1. Make people visualize how they will benefit, if they own the good or service offered, letting a dream come true.

2. Position the item in people's mind, as if they already own it, and they simply need to claim it. Once the ownership effect comes into play, message them if they don't take it, they will lose it. Give a free trial or sample of a product, and make customers own this, which makes the sample valuable. Once they own a product or a service, they don't want to lose it. For instance, Netflix, Spotify and Evernote offer free trials, nudging you to subscribe for avoiding the loss.

3. Discounts and coupons mention a specific gain turning into a loss. Pre-order deals not only offer discount and bonuses but also early exclusive access. Reward programs create a new currency that customers can exchange for products and services, and save money.

4. Urgency also stirs up fear of loss because if the customers don't avail the offer in time, they will lose all benefits. Many websites like Amazon display a countdown clock for deals of the day.

5. Scarcity adds to the fear of missing out by announcing that only limited quantities of the items are left. If a customer does not act fast, she will miss the chance of buying the item at a low price.

6. Social proof is added about how other customers are doing the same, using people's tendency to be influenced by others and keep up with the trend.

Choosing under certainty and uncertainty

We have an inbuilt desire for avoiding ambiguity, seeing patterns, and finding a reference. The lure of 100% is too much for us to ignore while deciding. The two natural reference points for something to occur are either its happening or not happening. The equivalent chances are 100 % if it happens or 0% if it does not happen. Our default mental habit, which uses less effort, is to lean towards 0 % or 100 %.

Let's say you are presented with two options:

1. $1 million for sure;

2.   A gamble with following chances of winning:
      a.   1% chance of $ 0
      b.   89% chance of $1 million
      c.   10% chance of $ 5 million

What will you choose?

Again you are presented with two options:

1.   A gamble with following chances of winning:
      a.   89% chance of $0;
      b.   11% chance of $ 1 million.
                  or
2.   A gamble with below chances:
      a.   90% chance of $0;
      b.   10% chance of $5 million

What do you choose?

Most people choose 1 over 2 in the first instance. It seems a no-brainer. Why would you not choose the safe, certain and 100% sure option of $1 million. After all, taking a risk for winning $5 million, you may land up not winning anything at all and is not worth risking sure shot $1 million.

In the second instance, people choose option 2 over 1. Now there are no certainties, no guarantees and no safe options. In fact, in either of the options, you may not win anything at all.

You are willing to take an extra 1% risk of having nothing for having a 10% chance at $5 million. If that be so why did you not choose option 2 over 1 in the first instance. Most people ignore the extra risk in favor of the size of the win.

As we move away from natural reference points of 0% and 100%, we move from certainty to probability, muddling our thinking. We have a preference for absolutes, which is actually a preference for the known, and anything between 0% and 100% does not really make sense to most people. On hearing about a 70% or 80% or 90% chance, we only infer one thing—no certainty, but likely.

Moreover, the psychological impact is much larger when we reduce the chance of happening something from certainty than from uncertainty. The effect of reducing a chance from 100% to 90% is much larger than reducing it from 90% to 80%, though the reduction in chance is same, 10%. Moving from certainty to uncertainty affects our decision making.

You are offered four soaps for the price of three. The alternative offer is buy three, get one free. What do you feel more certain about? Savvy marketers know how to present the offer.

Advantages of loss aversion

Loss aversion is powerful; it induces a psychological inertia. To change the state of inertia, we are reluctant to exert ourselves and instead go with our tendency toward maintaining status quo. This, however, can be used for advantage of society at large.

Most countries face a shortage of organ donors, while a number of patients die as they are on the wait list. In the United States alone, around 18 people die every day for want of an organ transplant.

Countries with laws on organ donations can broadly be classified in two types: opt-in countries and opt-out countries. In countries like United States and Germany, citizens must explicitly "opt in" for donating their organs when they die. In these opt-in countries, fewer than 15% of people register. On the other hand, in opt-out countries like Austria, organ donation is the default option at the time of death, and citizens must explicitly "opt out" of organ donation. In these countries, more than 90% citizens donate their organs.

In either countries, people prefer to maintain status quo. Opt-in countries like United States would do well to change the default option in favor of organ donation and save thousands of lives.

Recently, England changed its law around organ donation. The new system came into effect from 20 May 2020. Under the new 'opt out' system, all adults in England are presumed to have agreed to be an organ donor when they die, unless they decide not to donate or are in one of the excluded groups.

A person who does not want to donate, has to record her decision on the National Health Service (NHS) Organ Donor Register. It can be done online, or by calling on the contact center. But this requires effort for overcoming inertia, and most people are averse to do so.

Action tips: How to curb the impulse of loss aversion?

Overcoming loss aversion leads to better opportunities in life in general. We need to know when to do something as well when not to do something. Being an inherent tendency, we need to overcome it.

1. **Check your mindset**: Are you in a defensive mindset, caring more about not failing rather than winning? Do you place a very high value on losses compared to gains? If you are more afraid of losing things you already have than gaining new ones, then your fear of failure will overpower the will to win.

2. **Focus on both upside and downside**: Do not focus unduly on risks alone, exaggerating them, leaving out the rewards. If you want two to three times gains for an equivalent loss, then you are already in the grip of fear of failure.

3. **Don't push too hard**: In many situations, which involve change or uncertainty, don't push people too hard to choose in a short time. Let them be comfortable with your offer and not go into a loss aversion mindset. If pressed to answer yes or no, they may perceive the situation as too risky, by focusing on what they will be foregoing.

4. **Be realistic in assessing value**: While decluttering, view each item as if you don't own it. Now ask yourself, how much would you be willing to pay to buy it. Don't overvalue an item just because you own it. After gaining clarity on the utility of the item, it will be easier to let go of the item.

5. **Notice free trials and refund offers**: Marketers offer free trials of their products and full money back guarantees with no questions asked. This not only signals confidence in their products but also counters your fear of loss.

6. **Don't be pressured by deadline**: Sellers offer limited-time offers by setting a deadline and creating a sense of urgency in the prospective customers making

them not want to miss a good offer. Don't fall prey to this tactic.

7. **Beware of artificial scarcity**: Creating highly exclusive and limited run editions achieve the effect of scarcity, using the loss aversion to advantage.

8. **Know the probability**: Don't decide based only on absolutes, i.e., 0% or 100%, to avoid losses. Distinguish the real difference between 70% and 80%, where you can. Try to find the range of chances for ambiguous situations.

9. **Look for leverage**: Do not get stuck to certainty and let go of opportunities with less certainty but high upside, relative to the effort.

Quick Recap

- Our mind has an illogical habit to think losses are bigger than similar sized gains due to higher emotional value attached to a loss. Losing $50 will make you sadder than gaining $50 will make you happy.
- In realm of gains, we avoid risks; whereas in realm of losses, we prefer risk taking.
- Our gains and losses are defined relative to a reference.
- We have a natural preference for 0% and 100%, certainty or uncertainty, as reference points.
- Reducing something from certainty to uncertainty, i.e., 100% to 90% has a greater impact than reducing further from uncertainty, say, 90% to 80%.
- If fixated with certainty, we may let go of opportunities that have a high upside relative to effort.

Rewiring

After completing the exercises in the Action Guide under Rewiring: 5, you should know your tendency to behave when faced with gains and losses. You should also be aware of your habit in face of certainty as well uncertainty. Make your own action plan to counter the habit of loss aversion as per the 9 Action Tips above.

6

You have been framed!

"Things are not always what they seem; the first appearance deceives many; the intelligence of a few perceives what has been carefully hidden." – Phaedrus.

The legend of 17

"**B**y the third day of their honeymoon in Las Vegas the newlyweds had lost their $1,000 gambling allowance.

"That night the groom noticed a glowing object on the dresser. Upon closer inspection he realized it was a $5 chip they had saved as a souvenir.

"The number 17 was flashing brightly on the face of the chip.

"Taking this as an omen, he put on his green bathrobe and rushed down to the roulette table where, not surprisingly, he used the $5 chip to bet on number 17. It came in.

"He kept playing the number 17, letting his winnings ride. Eventually he was worth $7.5 million. Unfortunately, the floor manager intervened, claiming the casino didn't have the money to pay should 17 win again.

"So, the groom caught a taxi to another casino where he bet all on 17 again. When it hit he was worth $262m.

"Needless to say, with such luck he bet again, only to lose it all when the ball fell on 18.

"Broke and dejected, the groom walked miles back to his hotel.

'Where were you?' asked his wife.

'Playing roulette!' he replied. 'How did you do?' 'Not bad, I lost $5.'

If focused, then refocus

You are in the midst of Covid 19 pandemic, and you are as scared as anybody else. Wishing to take all precautions, you visit your local medicine store or pharmacy for buying a hand sanitizer. With stock running out of shelves, you spot two hand sanitizer bottles. One is Clean All and another is Clean It, both priced similar. The label on the Clean All states it kills 99% of germs, whereas the label on the Clean It claims it's very effective, only 1% of germs survive.

If you are like most people, you will end up buying Clean All as it appears more attractive. You would not like 1% germs to remain on your hands. The positive framing by Clean All wins over the negative framing of Clean It.

Simplest framing is glass half-full of water versus glass half-empty, as self-help books point out to us. The glass contains the same amount of water. What do we focus on? In buying sanitizer we focused on the element of risk as we chose between the two options.

Similarly, '90 % sugar free' sounds better than 'contains 10 % sugar'. Beef labelled as '75% lean' appears as higher quality than one with '25% fat'. Marketers know how our minds process information and frame an offer accordingly, focusing our attention on a specific feature.

Framing or fooling

Smart employers use this framing effect to reduce real wages during periods of price rises. Consider two scenarios:

Scenario 1: A company is making a small profit. It is located in a community experiencing a recession with high unemployment but no inflation. The company decides to decrease wages and salaries 7 percent this year.

The results of the survey are as follows:

Acceptable: 37 percent   Unfair: 63 percent

Scenario 2: A company is making a small profit. It is located in a community experiencing a recession with high unemployment and inflation of 12 percent. The company decides to increase salaries only 5 percent this year.

The results of the survey are as follows:

Acceptable: 78 percent   Unfair: 22 percent

If you understand inflation, you will know that inflation is the increase in price of goods. An inflation rate of 12 % means that what cost you $100 last year will cost you $112 this year. If your salary increases only by 5% against prices increasing by 12 %, you will end up paying 7 % more out of your pocket.

In the first scenario, the inflation remains same, i.e., whatever cost $100 last year will still cost the same this year but your salary has been decreased by 7%, so you will end up paying 7 % more from your pocket. In the second scenario, the inflation increases, i.e., whatever cost $100 last year will cost $112 this year but your salary has been increased only by 5%, so you will end up paying 7 % more from your pocket.

The power of framing is evident as scenario 1, which is framed as a nominal salary cut is judged as unfair. Whereas scenario 2 which is framed as a salary increase is judged as quite fair. The reality is opposite.

American Supreme Court Justice Oliver Wendell Holmes put it: "It is in the nature of a man's mind. A thing which you enjoyed and used as your own for a long time, whether property or opinion, takes root in your being and cannot be torn away without your resenting the act and trying to defend yourself, however you came by it. The law can ask no better justification than the deepest instincts of man."

Our view of the problem depends upon how the problem is framed and presented to us. The framing, in turn, decides the possible outcomes we can think of depending upon our personal characteristics and our consequent decision. However, all decision problems are not framed in a simple manner like the glass half-full or half-empty, which we can easily observe. We are presented with trickier options. Or worse still, options may be presented to us, which are actually not options at all.

Framing drives decisions

A policy may be presented to us, which appears beneficial for individuals, community, society or country at large. The option may be presented only in the context of one frame, the positive frame or the negative frame.

Consider you are the President of your country, and you have to decide the policy for containing a global pandemic like the Covid 19 caused by a new virus.

Frame 1(Survival frame): The outbreak due to the new virus is likely to kill 600,000 people. Public health experts have presented two alternative programmes:

If program A is implemented, 200,000 people will be saved.

If program B is implemented, there is a 33% chance that 600,000 people will be saved, and a 66% chance that nobody will be saved.

Which of the two programmes would you choose to implement.

More than 70% people choose program A. Notice that majority is risk-averse.

Frame 2 (Mortality frame): The outbreak due to the new virus is likely to kill 600,000 people. Public health experts have presented two alternative programmes:

If program C is implemented, 400,000 people will die.

If Program D is implemented, there is a 33% chance that nobody will die, and a 66% chance that 600,000 people will die.

Which of the two programmes would you choose to implement.

More than 78 % people choose program D and only 22 % chose program C, though program A and D are same, except for the framing. Outcomes are same, but phrased differently.

Did you notice the two frames? The first frame is Survival frame, starting from full mortality and shifting towards partial survival, presenting us the frame as a gain by saving lives. On the other hand, the second frame is Mortality frame, starting from full survival and shifting toward partial deaths, presenting the frame as a loss due to casualties. People are more likely to approve a policy that emphasizes survival rate than mortality rate. They will support an economic policy emphasizing rate of employment than the one emphasizing rate of unemployment.

A store displays a notice, informing about a discounted price, if you pay cash. However, if you pay via a credit card, you will have to pay an additional surcharge. No consumer would be willing to bear the cost of surcharge and forego a discount.

Even where no risk and loss or gain is involved, framing affects our mind. Performance of basketball players have been analyzed in terms of shots made, a positive frame, versus shots missed, a negative frame. Fans rated a player's performance better when the data was provided in terms of success rate than failure rate. And how would teachers rate the performance of students based on percentage questions answered correctly versus percentage questions answered incorrectly. You guessed it right. Students are judged better, if judged by percentage of questions answered correct.

Would a surgeon ever tell his patient that 5 out of every 100 patients undergoing surgery die, instead of telling that 95% of the patients undergoing surgery survive. Though both statements convey the same factual information, a doctor who does not want to scare his patients away would rather tell his patients that the survival rate for the surgery is 95%, using the frame of survival instead of frame of death.

Everyone agrees that cancer patients should be given alternatives for treatment and they should give an informed consent for any specific treatment. But the patient's decision depends upon how the alternatives are presented, knowingly or unknowingly. For most of the cancer patients, it is a tradeoff between quality and quantity of life. The frame, a positive one giving the probability of survival or a negative one giving the probability of dying, determines if the patient would be willing to undergo, say an aggressive chemotherapy, with side effects for prolonging his life or focus on the quality of life, in whatever remaining time he has left.

Choosing your reference point

The above decision-making problems presented a reference point, in terms of lives saved or lives lost, for us to take a decision. Often we pick our own reference points, and that too erroneous, perceiving the outcome as desirable or undesirable. We fool ourselves.

A punter who has been betting on horses has lost $ 140 at the bookmakers just before the close of the final race on the day. He entertains the thought to bet another $10 on a horse with 15:1 odds on the final race. With these odds, if the horse wins he gets $150, else if the horse loses, he loses $10.

Here the bettor can pick any of the two reference points. If the bettor includes the entire losses for the day until the final race, then either on winning the race he can recoup his loss of $140 or on losing the race he suffers a loss of $150. In this frame, the bettor is facing losses, and the last race of the day as an opportunity to breakeven will be quite attractive. He will be more risk-seeking and is likely to place the bet.

The bettor may choose another reference point by ignoring the prior losses taking them as sunk costs and not throw good money after bad money. With this perspective, the outcome of the last bet of the day could be either a gain of $150 or a loss of $10. In this frame of mind, the shift is from a gain to a loss and with a tendency to avert losses, the bettor may not place the bet. Once bitten twice shy.

Ignoring or including the previous results can affect our framing of the problem and related decisions. The larger frame is either of integration or segregation. Integrating some or all of the situations, events, and outcomes will change your reference point, putting you in a different frame of mind than if you were to segregate these outcomes.

Frame changes the color of money

It's all in the mind. We put different labels on money and spend it in foolish ways. Psychological accounting is an artificial construct in our minds, which we use to rationalize our decisions. We open separate accounts, keep a record, analyze, and even close them. We keep money in mental containers for various expenses like food, clothes, travel, housing, and entertainment. Similarly, we have accounts for income like salary, bonus, investment, and gifts.

Our bettor friend who started with an initial capital of $ 10 a fortnight ago has been lucky enough not only to recover his losses by breaking even, but also to post a profit of $150 by winning the next day as well. Chances are he will take this prior gain into account, when he decides his next betting amount, and he will bet more aggressively.

Gamblers in the casino exhibit a similar behavior as they are playing with the house money, the money from wins put in a separate mental account. The hard earned money is not being touched and under no threat of loss. After all, the reasoning goes, this additional money was never theirs to begin with. More often than not, money won from the house goes back to the house, as gamblers tend to risk more when they win. Under the impression of a hot hand, the winners end up losing all as the lucky streak comes to an end. No matter what game you play, chances of winning in a casino are very less as games are designed to provide an edge to the house.

The color of money is same, and it serves the same purpose whether you earned it by the sweat of your brow or won it in a lucky break or inherited it. The buying power of $100 remains the same, whether you find it on the road or earn it by the brow of your sweat. But while spending, we assign different values depending on its source. We take less care in spending what we find on road compared with what we earn on our job.

Investors on making larger than expected profits in the stock market may invest more recklessly after assigning a separate mental account for windfall gains. They will take risks which they avoid ordinarily. This was never my money, and I have got nothing to lose, says the voice in the head. Falling into a similar trap, most of the lottery winners go broke soon, squandering their millions. In America, the lottery winners are likely to become bankrupt within three to five years than the average American.

If you win the biggest lottery nobody expects you to continue with the same standard of living, but if you win modest amounts and squander them, then remember the old adage: a fool and his money are soon parted. Winnings from gambling and salary are not spent in a similar manner. The groom in the beginning of the chapter would have us believe that the winnings from the gambling were not real money or in any case, his money, and therefore, his loss of $262 million was not a real loss.

I can again hear you saying that you are not a gambling person and you have never ever visited a casino in your entire life. You never invest in stocks, never purchased a lottery ticket, and have never invested in bitcoins. After all you are a rational person, not a gambler or heir to a fortune, and you do not indulge in psychological accounting.

The illogic and emotion of mental accounting

Analyze the situation below and answer the following question in yes or no.

Situation 1: Imagine that you have decided to see a play, and you're planning to buy the $20 ticket when you arrive. As you enter the theater, you discover that you have lost $20 somewhere in the parking lot. Still you have enough money to buy the ticket. Would you pay $20 for another ticket?

After noting the response to above situation, analyze the situation below, and again respond with a yes or no.

Situation 2: Imagine that you have decided to see a play and have paid the admission price of $20 per ticket. As you enter the theater, you discover that you have lost the ticket. The seat was not marked, and the ticket cannot be recovered. Would you pay $20 for another ticket? Respond with a yes or no.

In the first situation, majority of people (88%) would buy a ticket as opposed to second situation wherein the majority (54%) said they would not buy a ticket. In terms of monetary loss, both situations are same: losing $20 in form of cash or theater ticket is immaterial. You have to think whether the play in the theater is worth watching for $20.

In situation 1, the loss of $20 is not subtracted from the mental account set up by the purchase of the ticket. By not linking the $20 loss to the ticket account, we do not exceed the mental budget for this account. In situation 2, the purchase of another ticket is subtracted from the mental account that was set up by the purchase of the original ticket. In this account, $40 is the cost of the ticket or cost of total entertainment to watch the play, which most of us find excessive.

A mental account may be temporary, as it is closed after the purpose is achieved such as buying a mobile phone or a house. Even where we have a choice to close an account we may not do so, if we feel that the account may be closed with a loss. Or we may close an account where we can close it with a profit, going by our propensity to feel losses more severely than gains. As in the previous chapter, the person whose portfolio witnesses a drop in value may not sell a specific stock that has gone down in price. By holding the stock, he can frame it as a paper loss, keeping the account open. Closing the account can be more painful.

Since money is fungible, $100 found on the roadside should be spent the same as a $100 from tax refund or $100 earned in salary. Just because you are spending a dollar from a separate mental bucket does not make it different. But it does not happen that way. Our mental categorization makes it non-fungible, setting rules for expenditure. Consolidating all accounts into one single account would be mentally taxing. Weighing every immediate transaction against the long-term benefits—watching a movie every month versus depositing $20 in the retirement plan would suck all the joy out of life. An entertainment account is not treated with the same seriousness as a retirement account. The lazy habit of mental accounting spares our brain the mental effort of comparing across all the categories. And our mind loves shortcuts.

At times, we also deposit the money into a wrong mental account. We tend to deposit tax refunds from the government into a found money account and splurge it. Tax refund is in effect a delayed payment of your earnings, and had you taken out the equivalent money from your salary and deposited in a bank account, you would not have touched it now. However, you are attaching a different value to the money due to a flawed mental accounting system.

Apart from this, we also treat money differently depending upon the amount of money in question or the size of the mental account or the size of the transaction.

Imagine that you go to a store to buy a suitcase, which sells for $99. At the store you discover that the same suitcase is on sale for $75 at a branch of the store five blocks away. Do you go to the other branch to get the lower price?

Now imagine that you go to the same store to buy a sofa set, which sells for $1,774. At the store you discover that you can buy the same sofa set for $1,750 at a branch of the store *five blocks away. Do you go to the other branch to get the lower price?*

Most of us will go to the other branch to save on the suitcase than would travel the same distance to save on the sofa set, even though we are faced with the same choice: Would you walk five blocks to save $24? Now, you know whom to blame. $24 seems a paltry sum relative to $1774. This habit to ignore small costs can cost dear in the long run.

Principles of mental accounting are anything but rational. If you get a small refund or bonus, say $200, you may put it in a mental account meant for consumption. You may buy a jacket for yourself. Whereas, if you were to receive a big sum, say $20,000, you will put it into a long-term account, making it harder to purchase a new jacket, though you can afford it comfortably.

Credit card companies utilize our tendency to treat money differently to the hilt. Money which we pay through plastic card is devalued in our mind, as we do not feel any loss at the time of purchase. In reality that money might be more valuable considering the high interest rate of 16% to 24 % charged by most credit card companies. Also, we are likely to spend more money when paying through a credit card than paying by cash.

However, the siloed approach to money also has its benefits. For instance, people do not touch retirement savings for routine expenditures or luxury vacations. If some people who are spendthrifts did not have mental accounts, they would never be able to pay their house mortgage or fund their children's education. And if you are prone to spending small sums of money and unable to save it, channel your money directly from your salary to a mutual fund or savings bank account.

So the best would be to use mental accounting to our benefit without succumbing to its harmful effects. But before that you need to know are you already a victim of mental accounting, blissfully unaware, and therefore, prone to wasting money.

Tips to check if you are a victim of mental accounting

1. You have a tendency to splurge with a tax refund than with savings.

2. You spend more while using credit cards than while using cash.

3. You don't consider yourself as an extravagant spender, but you have trouble saving.

4. You have savings in the bank and at the same time are carrying balances on your credit card from month to month.

Action tips: How to negate mental accounting?

1. **Imagine you are paying in cash**: Before buying anything on credit, pause for a moment and ask yourself, how much would you have paid, if you were paying cash out of your pocket. You may want to pay much less or even abandon the purchase altogether. This is better than cutting up your plastic credit cards.

2. **Break big ticket items into components**: When you purchase a high-cost item, break it into various major and minor components. Do you really need a car

with alloy wheels or with the high end stereo? $500 might look a paltry sum against $19,000 for a new car.

3. **Wait before spending windfall money**: If at all you get windfall money from a lottery, gift, inheritance or even tax refunds and bonuses, do not decide to spend it immediately. Let it be parked in a bank account or fixed deposit for a time period. You are free to do whatever you want to do after a few months. It's your money and not going anywhere; rather it will grow as it earns interest. You may change your plans or come up with a better plan and stop seeing it as found money. Beware of this, especially if you have won a lottery.

4. **View all income as earned income**: For dealing with money that you did not earn, ask yourself how much time and effort would you need to expend to earn that much amount of money after taxes. Once you value money in terms of hard work, you will view it equally.

Framing in marketing and selling

Insurance is a trillion-dollar industry across the world, its bedrock being the purchase of all types of insurance ranging from home to health, life to property to car and pets among others.

By now you know, your decision depends upon how the outcomes are framed. In choosing between a risky outcome and a certain outcome, the outcomes can be framed as either gains or losses, depending on the choice of reference point. Most of us choose a certain outcome with a gain frame and prefer the risky outcome with a loss frame.

Insurance companies selling life insurance do not emphasize the frame of mortality. Rather they associate positive emotions with insurance products, for instance, 'Adding life to insurance' or 'Life insured by care.'

A savvy marketer depending upon the context would inform his prospective customers that using his product everyday would cost him less than two dollars a day rather than cost $729 a year. Marketers pick up the best frame based upon the target segment and the available information. The frames could range from the usual gain and loss to providing value and achieving personal goals to desirability and power to positive and negative. Frames become more potent when combined.

Sales and marketing personnel also use human's innate aversion to extremeness. While making purchases, customers are provided with three options: cheaper, mid-range and expensive. The majority chooses the mid-range option, the seller increasing its margins with respect to the cheaper option. Marketers play upon our tendency to avoid extreme option and choose an intermediate option by placing the extreme alternative such that the target alternative is placed at the center of the triad.

Framing the price options in such a manner almost forcing the customer to choose a particular product is also known as decoy pricing. Let us say a business is selling two types of coffeemakers priced at $ 30 and $60, with margins of $10 and $ 25 respectively. A third coffeemaker, a decoy, is launched by the company priced at $100, margin being $60. The high-end coffee maker will not register much sales, but will boost sales of the mid-range coffee maker. Many of our decisions are based on our tendency to avoid extreme choices, choosing the mid-range option when we have a choice from three.

Framing in policy making

Once we know framing can lead to different behaviors, we need to understand if framing is distorting our perception.

Can we discard the frame and look at the bare information as such to avoid getting manipulated by frames?

Ultimately framing is about communication and we rely a lot on metaphors while communicating. Very subtle framing by use of metaphors can change our views on policy matters.

For instance, in a city grappling with crime, becoming increasingly unsafe due to theft, robberies, and murder, the answer may depend upon the metaphor that describes the problem. If crime is described as a "beast" preying on a community, then citizens support augmenting police force and jailing offenders. However, if people are told crime is a "virus" infecting a city, then they prefer to treat the problem with social reform.

A study carried out in the fictional city of Addison provided crime reports to the participants containing disturbing statistics how 10,000 more crimes were reported in the preceding three-year period, and how the murders had gone up from 330 to 550 in the same period.

When people were asked what influenced them the most, very few mentioned the metaphor, and the majority said their suggestion to curb crime was swayed by statistics. Though the metaphor framed their decision, they believed it was objective, logical, and decided on data.

Those who read the frame, "Crime is a beast ravaging the city of Addison" were 20 % more likely to support strengthening law enforcement than who read the alternative frame, "Crime is a virus ravaging the city of Addison", irrespective of their political leanings.

This leads us to another conclusion. Smart politicians do not have to polarize the electorate for garnering support on various issues, instead they can frame the message through the right metaphors.

Framing in politics

On May 12, 1975 Khmer Rouge regime in Cambodia seized SS Mayaguez, a U.S container ship along with 39 crew members. The crew were held hostage on the Cambodian island of Koh Tang. President Gerald Ford ordered the marines to launch a mission for rescuing the crew from the island. Soon after the attack on the island, the Cambodians transferred the crew to the mainland. The marines to their surprise encountered elite Khmer Rouge troops, and a bitter battle ensued. The U.S. bombed the mainland. The Mayaguez was recovered, and its crew were released by the Cambodians, not rescued by the marines, a fact not brought out by the President while announcing victory.

In the end, 41 American soldiers had been killed, 50 wounded, and three CH-53 helicopters shot down. Moreover, three marines who had been left behind in the fog of battle were captured and executed by Khmer Rouge. A diplomatic crisis erupted as U.S had used a base in Thailand for launching the rescue mission. By all standards, this was a botched operation.

Yet the way the episode was framed it was perceived to be a success by the public. In one poll, 79% of the people rated President Ford's handling of the incident very high. In fact, when Ford ran for reelection in 1976, rather than regretting it, he highlighted the incident.

17 years later, another U.S. President George H. W. Bush sent military to Somalia, a state ripped asunder with civil war and starvation. Known as Operation Restore Hope, the aim was noble: securing humanitarian aid to the African state during the years 1992-1994. The UN and the International Red Cross' efforts were stymied by the political chaos in Somalia as aid workers and convoys were attacked frequently. By December 1992, when the U.S. military started arriving in Somalia, 3,000 people were starving to death every day.

As it happens in military operations, surprises sprang up, and in an unexpected turn of events a team of Delta Force and U.S. Rangers found themselves involved in capture of Somali Warlord General Mohammed Farah Aidid's associates. The routine manhunt operation supposed to last for an hour led to a prolonged and pitched battle in the streets of Somalian capital, Mogadishu. Between 3 and 4 October, the Americans lost 18 soldiers, 80 were wounded, and two Black Hawk helicopters were shot down. In military terms, the U.S. soldiers decimated the warlord's forces, killing around 1000 members, militia suffering a 50-to-1 casualty ratio.

After the battle in Mogadishu, President Clinton's approval ratings of his handling the Somalian crisis fell to 30 percent. Till date, the U. S. intervention is remembered more for Black Hawk Down incident, made into a Hollywood movie, and less for saving a million lives from violence or famine to halving the number of refugees to building infrastructure during the entire two-year period. Despite several successes, the dominant perception of this complex and multifaceted operation is of a disastrous failure.

Compare a failed Mayaguez operation framed as a success and the Somalian operation with many accomplishments framed as a debacle. Therefore, framing is important in political communication: a leader wanting to continue in office has to be seen to be winning.

Smart politicians frame poor information or lesser options in a positive manner, making them more attractive than other actually better options or information.

The order of information matters

The Trappist monks practice extreme austerity. The story about the monks though apocryphal brings out the power of framing.

Monk 1 asked his abbot whether it would be all right to smoke while he prayed. Scandalized, the abbot said, "Of course not; that borders on sacrilege." Monk 2 asked his abbot whether it would be all right to pray while he smoked. "Of course," said the abbot, "God wants to hear from us at any time."

How we perceive, comprehend, and interpret world around us is influenced not just by the habitual thought patterns that are activated in particular contexts, but by the framing of judgments we have to make. The order in which we encounter information of various kinds is one kind of framing. Monk 2 was well aware of the importance of order of input for framing his request.

Action tips: How to nullify framing?

Other people do not see the problem through the same frame as we do. For escaping the framing effect, do the following when faced with a situation or presented with a choice option:

1. **Identify the frame**: Is it about two risk choices or a specific feature being highlighted, especially in terms of loss or gain? Is the framing trying to persuade you to behave or not behave in a particular manner? Is the issue being framed positively or negatively. Are you thinking of avoiding the loss?

2. **View differently**: Look for different perspectives. View it in the opposite frame.

3. **Check the reference point**: Check if the reference point includes some or all of the outcomes and events. View the situation from different reference points.

4. **Look for further details**: Increase your level of involvement, and go into details. Are the outcomes same but worded differently? Seemingly innocuous changes in words can have significant consequences.

5. **Reframe**: Discard the initial frame, and then reframe in various ways without undue emphasis on any one aspect. Changing the frame often changes the decision.

Quick Recap

- We make and justify decisions based on the way they are framed instead of bare facts. Hence, framing can be dangerous.
- Choices are generally framed highlighting gains or losses, choosing between two risky options, emphasizing one particular feature, or positive versus negative effects.
- How something is said becomes more important than what is said, leading us to select an option that emphasizes positive features or averts losses.
- We prefer the low-risk option in the positive frame and a risky alternative in the negative frame.
- Your decision is a combination of the way problem is presented, your perception, and personal traits.
- By labelling money differently in various mental accounts, we tend to spend easily and foolishly, especially small sums of money.

Rewiring

Complete the exercises in the Action Guide under Rewiring: 6. You should be able to safeguard against framing as well against mental accounting.

7

Cut Your Losses Than Be Pigheaded

You've got to know when to hold 'em

Know when to fold 'em

Know when to walk away

And know when to run...

Kenny Rogers, The Gambler

Concorde fallacy

Concorde could fly non-stop across the Atlantic Ocean, reaching Paris from New York in less than three and a half-hour. First flown in 1969, the supersonic passenger airliner was a technological leap, flying at more than twice the speed of sound. The subsonic commercial jets took eight hours for the same run.

Flying at Mach 2, the Concord or Le Concorde, was an Anglo-French collaboration. From 1962, the time the British and the French governments had signed an accord, to 1975, when the bookings began for the commercial services, the project went through many ups and downs, and more importantly, the world had changed substantially.

Concorde consumed four times the fuel than a Boeing 747 on the New York-Paris route. Oil prices quadrupled in 1973, affecting its commercial viability vis-à-vis the sub-sonic jets. Airlines were laying more emphasis on being superefficient than superfast.

Beset by design and technical issues, its commercial deployment was delayed by at least five years. By 1975, many American airlines, large potential buyers for the jet, were planning to buy the new jets produced by domestic manufacturers. The market for faster passenger travel was not as huge as anticipated, and the segment remained a niche. The surge in passenger traffic in the previous years was a result of the increase in the number of tourists, but they could not afford to pay for prices higher than first-class tickets of subsonic passenger aircraft.

Apart from time overruns, the cost overruns while building the Concorde were tremendous. A New York Times article in 1979 stated that since 1962 the estimates were revised at least six times until then. The original project was to cost 160 million GBP but even just before its commercial launch it had spent 1.2 billion GBP.

The losses continued after that and Concorde was finally grounded in 2003. The supersonic passenger travel may have come to an end but not the losses due to the sunk costs.

To be fair, confidential memorandum of the British government in 29 November 1971, now declassified, noted,' Concorde is a commercial disaster....... The decision whether or not to abandon Concorde must start from where we are now—much of the milk is already spilt.' Despite accurate understanding of the sunk costs in the project, it was a political decision to continue for avoiding embarrassment and maintaining prestige. It was also a part of the British Foreign Office's strategy to gain entry to the European Common Market.

The Concorde fallacy itself may be a fallacy. So much so, that the Concorde project has become synonymous with sunk cost phenomenon also known as Concorde fallacy. Richard Dawkins, a famous evolutionary biologist, wrote a paper titled, 'Do digger wasps commit the Concorde Fallacy'? He was investigating the tendency of wasps to invest large amount of resources in defending their nests, whereas it would be less costly to build a new nest.

The Nokia fiasco

If you thought public sector is notorious for wasteful expenditure by ignoring sunk costs, then corporations are no better. But a project often continues to avoid humiliation and political implications, or for sheer strategic considerations. More often than not, leaders feel their reputation is invested in it.

Nokia was the dominant market leader in mobile phones in 2008 with almost 40% global market share. Yet within a span of five years, it had to divest its entire mobile phone business unit to Microsoft in 2013. Symbian software was the leading mobile operating system before 2007 and the most crucial technological factor in the rise of Nokia in the early 2000s. Nokia acquired full ownership of Symbian Limited. The firm invested too much in resources and market technology specific to Symbian, escalating its commitment. However, the competitive environment changed drastically as smartphones like Apple with its iOS and Google's open source android OS entered the market. But Nokia was busy releasing Ovi updates till the fag end.

Nokia's executives wanted to recoup losses at any cost, somehow save face, and prove that they were right all along. They fell deep into the pit of sunk cost.

Labelling a cost as a sunk cost itself gives rise to disagreement among team members. Another way to look at it is to see if a cost changes due to change in business activity. If it is a sunk cost, it will not. It is independent of future costs that may be incurred. Money that has already been spent cannot be recovered.

Where financial profitability is the criteria for continuation of a project, a cost-benefit analysis, comparing the future costs against anticipated benefits can provide inputs on whether to continue or terminate a project. At whichever point we are in the lifecycle, we do not take past costs or benefits into account.

Fundamental to this is the choice between abandoning the project to cut your losses or continuing ahead in the hope of recouping losses. Often, hope triumphs over reality for a variety of reasons.

Pyrrhic victory in wars

In long-drawn wars with victory not in sight, nations continue to fight as they cannot forget the sacrifices of their valiant soldiers and make sure that their boys did not die in vain. Americans took so long to withdraw from Vietnam in the 1960s. After spending millions of dollars and losing thousands of lives, if the United States withdrew from Vietnam without achieving its objectives, then these sacrifices would go waste was the argument.

The lesson was clear: while fighting a losing battle, do not double down, instead cut your losses. Otherwise you only double your losses. Either it wasn't learnt well or forgotten too soon.

The Soviets justified their quagmire in Afghanistan in the 1980s on similar grounds. In 2006, President Bush gave various reasons for staying the course in Iraq. One of them was "not going to allow the sacrifice of 2,527 troops who have died in Iraq to be in vain by pulling out before the job is done."

President Trump on American involvement in Afghanistan said, "Our nation must seek an honorable and enduring outcome worthy of the tremendous sacrifices that have been made, especially the sacrifices of lives. The men and women who serve our nation in combat deserve a plan for victory".

We owe it to the dead and wounded; withdrawal will cheapen the lives of those already sacrificed; and, the dead have not died in vain are powerful emotional arguments. Often there may be reasons to continue with a war; however, letting more soldiers die to justify those already dead may avoid a feeling of failure, but is bad reasoning. Soldiers who are already dead will remain dead, whether a nation achieves its objectives or not. This cannot be the reason for staying the course, or withdrawing, or favoring one course of action over the other. The decision has to be based on today's situation.

Death on Mount Everest

10 May 1996: Camp IV, Mount Everest, Nepal

Come what may, Doug Hansen, an old postal worker from Washington, was determined to climb the world's highest mountain peak this time in 1996. Reaching the summit of Mount Everest requires skill, grit, and luck. Above all, it requires a clear head too.

A year earlier in 1995, the expedition leader Hall had turned him away just 330 vertical feet from the summit. In Hall's estimate, had Doug reached the summit, he would not have been able to reach back in time before he ran out of supplementary oxygen.

This time, many other climbers were on their way to reach the pinnacle as part of two separate expeditions, one of which was led by Hall and the other by Fisher. Most of the participants had spent years mountaineering and trekking, and specifically endured weeks of gruelling training, acclimatizing for this ascent. Each had spent around $

70,000 for this expedition alone. A huge amount of time, money, and effort were already invested.

The final leg, from Camp IV to the peak, was 18 hours long. Crucial to reaching the summit and back to Camp IV was reaching the peak just after noon, no later than 1 or 2 p.m. Otherwise, the climbers would be descending late into the night and were sure to run out of supplemental oxygen. Therefore, once the climbers realised that they would not be able to reach the top by mid-afternoon, they would need to turn around, an unwritten standard operating procedure(SOP) based on experience. But the mountaineers are reluctant to do so.

'I've put too much of myself into this mountain to quit now without giving it everything I've got,' said Doug Hansen, just before the final ascent. And he reached the summit but only after 4 p.m. This time Hall did not turn him around, and many other climbers were loath to turn back so near to the goal.

The weather started worsening during the descent, and soon enough all the mountaineers were caught in a blizzard. A total of eight people including Hall, Doug died on the descent, making it one of the deadliest season in the history of Mount Everest. Only the three who had returned survived.

Books have been written about the disastrous expedition and a Hollywood movie, Into Thin Air, made on the subject. Apart from other logistical failures that led to delays, it was the mind set of escalating commitment that drove the disaster. It is human nature to not withdraw after investing huge amount of resources in a task, despite negative outcomes in successive stages.

In the best of times, climbing Mount Everest requires clear thinking. But at 27,000 feet and above, air is in short supply and climbers hallucinate due to lack of oxygen at high altitude, often getting disoriented. Getting weighed down by sunk costs in such a state can lead to wrong decisions, making the difference between life and death.

Like Francesco Schettino, the captain of cruise ship, Hall and Fischer were experienced and overconfident. They had reasons to do so. They had climbed world's toughest mountains. Hall had scaled to the summit four times and guided 39 clients to the Everest.

Both had impressive track records and had emerged victorious in face of odds on numerous occasions. Fischer felt he had 'built a yellow brick road to the summit', and his wife wasn't concerned about him at all when he was guiding because he was going to make all the right choices. Hall was no less brimming with overconfidence as he felt 'he could get almost any reasonably fit person to the summit'.

Sunk costs of time, effort, and love

At times, even with complete oxygen on ground, we build castles in the air or decide to pursue a course in the name of strategic considerations.

It is not only teams and group that fall prey to not factoring sunk costs. In our individual capacities, we fare no better. Once we have committed time, we only escalate a commitment. If you have been waiting at the bus stop for half an hour, you tend to wait for another 10 minutes, then another 5 minutes, and so on. Even after 45 minutes the bus does not arrive, but since you have invested so much time you decide to wait for another 15 minutes as the bus may arrive any moment. The chance of a bus arriving is not dependent upon how much time you have already waited for. That time is a sunk cost.

We keep on watching a movie because we purchased the tickets, drove to the theatre, have already sat through for an hour, and seen half of it. We do this despite not wanting to do so, otherwise we feel we are wasting money spent on purchasing the ticket. We do not realise money is already wasted as we are not enjoying the movie. On top of that we are also wasting time. When choosing between wasting only money, and both time and money, we choose the latter. Setting aside the regret, our decision in the middle of the boring movie should be based on whether we want to see the movie at all, irrespective of the price. For a similar reason, we keep on reading a boring book.

Or let us check this out. It's Sunday morning, and you are thinking how to spend the evening. You may watch a movie in the theatre, or cook yourself a lovely dinner and stay at home. After thinking a bit, you decide that you would enjoy cooking a meal yourself and staying at home, rather than going to the theatre. So you decide to stay at home. Later in the afternoon, you suddenly remember that you had purchased the ticket to the movie theatre a month ago for $100, price being quite high by your standards.

The ticket is non-refundable, and it's too late to resell it or give it away. Not attending the movie show tonight means the expensive ticket goes to waste. Would you be more likely to watch the movie show after realising that you have invested a fairly high amount in it? Would you watch the movie, if the ticket was given to you for free?

If you are likely to watch the movie because of your investment in buying the ticket, then you are honoring sunk costs.

Take a famous example. One basketball fan purchases a costly ticket for the upcoming match, and another gets a free ticket well before the day of the match. Around the time of the match, a snow storm happens. The person who paid for the ticket drives down to the venue, putting himself in considerable danger, as he did not want to waste the money. Whereas the other person stayed at home as he felt he would not be wasting anything.

You visit a restaurant, order food, but continue to gorge on it even after feeling full because you have paid for it and can't waste the food. All this sounds bizarre and illogical, yet all of us have fallen prey to it sometime or the other.

Sunk costs need not be only of money; they can be of time or efforts in our personal lives as well. We persist with our goals, simply because we have already invested huge resources.

People continue to date somebody or tolerate other relationship as so much time and emotions have been invested, even though the things are not working out the way they want it to be. Such people have passed a mental point of no return of their own making, feeling locked in due to prior investment. They pursue the path, even if it is not in their best interest.

You spent $700 on your 11-year old car a week ago. It seems you need to spend another $1000 to keep it running. Since you have already sunk $700, you continue to spend on it. After all you need to get your money's worth. You cannot scrap it just like that. The more money, time, or effort we invest in something, the harder it is to let go.

Coupled with this we have another tendency to seem consistent with our earlier commitments, ideas, words and actions, even if it harms us. If we have committed publicly, then it becomes even more difficult for us to change our course of action.

Sales persons are adept in securing a small commitment, a toe-in-the-door, and then escalating it.

Opportunity cost

In life, at work and at play, you are faced with a multitude of opportunities. However, you cannot make use of all these opportunities, and you need to choose. Each choice, each decision carries an associated cost. You also incur a loss, when you take one action instead of an alternative action.

Opportunity cost is the cost of what you give up, to get something else. It's the cost of the foregone alternative. It does not include any monetary payment, as it is unseen. It makes you aware of the set of choices you have, and are you exercising the best choice.

When you decide to go to college, apart from tuition fees the true cost of college would include the opportunity cost of wages that you could have earned, if you had not decided to go to college. That's why you will prefer to join college at a younger age, when your earnings from salary are relatively low. For working professionals, executive MBA programmes, or part time programmes hold great charm. In fact, one-year MBA programmes are popular than two-year programmes because the opportunity costs in terms of earnings foregone and time invested are lesser.

It can also be viewed in terms of value foregone and physical quantity given up, which differ on the basis of personal feelings, tastes, or opinions.

Sunk costs are backward looking, and, in contrast, opportunity costs are forward looking. Opportunity costs at the time of decision making are fixed and identified looking forward. They cannot be changed with retrospective effect. Viewing opportunity costs in hindsight can only give you insights in the process of decision making for future. For instance, looking back the next-best option may have been the best option, or choices were not as few as thought at the time of decision.

When the French and British governments continued footing the bill for Concorde, they restrained funds for potentially lucrative subsonics, including the French Caravelle and the European Airbus aircraft. And they did pay a high opportunity cost.

Opportunity costs are not considered in isolation of other factors impinging on your decision making. Two stocks having the same opportunity cost may have different risks, and the probabilities of various outcome may be different. These can also compound over a period of time. Buying a latte from Starbucks costing $ 2.95 may not amount to much, but if you buy one every day for next 20 years, with the sheer power of compounding at 4 % it adds up to $ 33,621. Of course, we do not analyse our daily choices from this perspective.

You may be an IT worker in Oslo, and, say, you are offered a job in New York with a slightly higher salary. You decide to leave green, transport friendly Oslo for expensive, crowded New York with traffic jams. The opportunity cost of higher salary is poor quality of life.

For a child who decides to attend after-school football classes, the opportunity cost is forgoing piano lessons. By now you would have realized, opportunity costs involve sacrifice as the alternatives are mutually exclusive; no sacrifice means no opportunity cost. If you decide to take a day off from work to see a sports match, then the opportunity cost   is the cost of ticket for the match in addition to the money you would have earned had you not missed work.

Even discerning voters support government programmes after weighing their benefits and costs, while omitting opportunity costs. If public opinion polls were to highlight opportunity costs, the public support for the government policies related to taxation and other spending would undergo a change.

Did you notice that the moment you honour sunk costs you end up paying unnecessary opportunity cost? We can't have it all. Intuitively, we understand when we say don't throw good money after bad money and that 'you can do anything but you cannot do everything'.

Accepting sunk costs means agreeing that you have wasted your time, money or effort, without getting a commensurate return on it. You have paid the cost, and it cannot be recovered.

It seems preposterous that we would risk more time, money, or resources on a project or a personal task that is doomed. But all of us irrespective of our economic status, experience, and cultural background fall prey to sunk cost phenomenon. It is universal and widespread.

Action tips: How to evade pitfall of sunk cost?

1. **Accept losses**: Check if you are continuing with a project because you need to get your money or time's worth and do not want to appear wasteful.

2. **Compulsion to be consistent**: Accepting sunk costs may mean a change of direction and decision than before. Are you afraid that your image may take a beating, and you may come across as fickle, weak and unreliable? Is it your ego? Is a stigma of failure lurking in your mind and making you cling to your original decision?

3. **Link with opportunity cost**: Just by persisting in the old course of action, are you paying a high price in the long run by foregoing the next best option.

4. **Visualize a future scenario**: Revisit your main goal or strategy. Check, if it would be better to cut your losses now rather incur greater losses at a later date. Maybe in the longer run, accepting losses today won't matter.

5. **Seek independent opinion**: Look at the events as an independent third party or as an outsider to get an impartial opinion. Let the project be reviewed by somebody,

who is not a part of the team. In case of a personal matter, take advice from somebody whom you trust.

6. **Decide the rules**: Whether it's a project or personal financial investment or your relationships, decide the rules, limits, and redlines beforehand. This way you will know, when to cut your losses and avoid falling into the trap.

Quick Recap

Sunk costs

- An expense of time, effort, or money already invested in something that cannot be recovered.
- When we continue with the task by putting value on how much we have already invested, instead of analysing the costs and benefits as on today, we further increase our losses.

Opportunity costs

- The cost of next best alternative that is sacrificed, i.e. what you give up to do what you want. These costs are unseen.

Rewiring

Refer exercises in the Action Guide under Rewiring: 7. You should be aware, if you are already in the mental trap of sunk costs and be able to calculate opportunity costs.

8

First Impression is the Last Impression

"The answer is that we are not helpless in the face of our first impressions. They may bubble up from the unconscious - from behind a locked door inside of our brain - but just because something is outside of awareness doesn't mean it's outside of control".
Malcolm Gladwell

A gruesome murder that has made national headlines all across print, electronic, and social media is tried in a court. Lawyers arguing from both prosecutor and defendant's side have spoken passionately, and all witnesses have deposed in front of the judge. It's time for lunch, and the judgement will be pronounced after the court reassembles in an hour.

Imagine you are the judge, and you have an hour's time to finish lunch and decide about the period of sentence as well. You go through the case once again, noticing the significant facts. The evidence is mixed, and you can't really make up your mind about how many years the defendant should be sentenced. You also remember the words of a journalist asking you, if the sentence would be higher or lower than 10 years. You mull over the 10-year sentence as being too harsh or lenient. Do you think the journalists question would influence your decision?

If the answer is yes, you are in distinguished company of judges and subject to anchoring. If the answer is no, you are a rare exception.

Anchoring of your mind is much like the anchor of a ship when lowered prevents the ship from moving away. It fastens you to a position. Numeric anchoring is the most pervasive phenomenon, fixating us to a particular number.

Anchors come in a wide variety

In a study, the judges were given a case of murder, wherein the accused had stabbed a man to death who was having an affair with his fiancée. Half the judges were requested to sentence the man in years, and the remaining half were requested to sentence in months. The judges that sentenced in years awarded the accused a 9.7-year prison term. Those who sentenced in months awarded 5.7 years in prison to the accused, a decrease of 43.3 % compared to sentence in months. Though 12 months and 1 year are same, the number 12 is larger and seems extreme than the number 1. A judge becomes anchored to sentence expressed in months, bringing down the total sentence. Male and female judges were affected equally by the bias.

Not only in decision making but also in the realm of estimating, we are likely to be weighed down by anchors. Consider the result of multiplying numbers one to eight as given below for not more than five seconds:

$$1 \times 2 \times 3 \times 4 \times 5 \times 6 \times 7 \times 8$$

Without formally calculating, note down your estimate. Generally, people estimate it around 512.

Now, instead of numbers being presented in an ascending sequence (1 × 2 × ... × 8) as done earlier, these are presented in a descending sequence:

$$8 \times 7 \times 6 \times 5 \times 4 \times 3 \times 2 \times 1$$

After transposing, the estimate is around 2,250.

Most of us who focus on the descending sequence 8 × 7 × 6 × 5 × 4 × 3 × 2 × 1 estimate that this string yields a higher result than the one in reverse order. The estimates are based on the product of first few numbers that act as an anchor, the product higher for the descending sequence than the ascending sequence. The correct answer is 40,320.

While estimating we generate our own anchors, quite relevant to the situation at hand. For instance, while estimating freezing point of 100 proof vodka, we may use freezing point of water as an anchor, adjusting it downwards as alcohol has lower freezing point than water. The freezing point of water is zero degrees Celsius or 32 degrees Fahrenheit. Would you like to estimate the freezing point of 100 proof vodka? Let me give you another tip: The higher the proof of alcohol, the lower the freezing point.

The freezing point of 100 proof vodka is -40.43 degrees Celsius or -40.78 degrees Fahrenheit.

In most of real life circumstances, we often fail to adjust enough to our initial anchor values. Even where the anchors are relevant and where we know the direction in which the benchmark value is to be adjusted, upwards or downwards, we tend to adjust insufficiently. Since we are uncertain about the true value, we move the answer away from the initial value until what seems a plausible range. As uncertainty increases, the plausible range increases, and, therefore, the adjustment is inadequate.

Precise anchors like 2.73 instead of 3 create bigger anchoring effects, especially as the anchor is perceived as informative. Also, we tend to adjust a general anchor like $ 150,000 more than $141,986. When faced with a general anchor, we adjust in larger increments compared to a specific anchor. For instance, we will adjust a general anchor like $30 in large increments like $31, $32, $29, whereas we will adjust a specific anchor like $28.35 on a lower scale like $28.45, $28.25 etc. Hence, due to the big anchoring effect of precise initial price, the final price in a negotiation will be closer to initial price.

How the absurd anchors us?

Can a mere suggestion trigger the anchoring process, no matter how trivial or irrelevant? Let me continue my obsession with legal system, courts, and judges as anchoring effects can mark the difference between life and death or the time spent in prison.

Junior judges in Germany were chosen for a study and were told to roll a dice for determining the prosecutor's demand for sentence. Half the judges were handed over a rigged dice that showed either of the numbers 1 and 2. The other half were given a loaded dice that always displayed either 3 or 6. After rolling the pair of dice, the judges were to sum the total of both the dice and enter into a questionnaire as the prosecutor's sentencing demand ranging from one to twelve months.

For identical crimes, the judges who were exposed to a high anchor awarded higher sentences, average 7.81 months, whereas judges exposed to a low anchor awarded lower sentences with average of 5.28 months. The difference means almost 50 % longer time spent in prison. Now you may say that judges do not throw dice before awarding prison sentences. But you would have realized judges' decision can be influenced by seemingly irrelevant anchors that are topmost in their minds and these, of course, need not be dice, but could be media, friends, family, or spouse.

While deciding, estimating, and forecasting, we rely on the initial piece of information offered to us, more so if it is in numeric form. And these effects can be transient as well as long lasting.

Dropping and countering anchor

Negotiations are complex affairs, and expert negotiators understand the power of anchoring. They make the first offer and anchor the talks with an idea or a number, tilting the balance in their favour. Similarly, if the counterpart gives the first offer, dropping an anchor, the pros know what to do.

Let us say you are negotiating to buy a house with a potential seller for which you have done your homework by surveying the market. You are not willing to pay more than $ 150,000 for the property. The seller drops an anchor by expressing his willingness to sell it for $ 200,000. You would do well not to respond immediately with your counter offer. Rather you would first negate the anchor set up the other party. It means telling the other party clearly, politely, and firmly that $200,000 is not acceptable to you. After this you would give your counter offer, taking care of not mentioning the initial anchor repeatedly, else you might validate it.

It is not, however, advantageous to make the first offer always. This will depend upon how much information is available, how prepared you are, and whether you are a seller or a buyer. The conventional wisdom still holds it is better never to make the first offer. But then you may fall prey to the risk of anchoring. So, try your best to ignore the anchor by not dwelling on it or changing the subject to manage the effect of anchoring.

The anchored friend

Most of us know of an acquaintance, a friend, a relative who got stuck with an anchor while buying or selling a house, ending up in a loss. Your uncle Joe would not sell his house for a penny less than $150,000 because the house in his neighbourhood had been sold for a similar amount. So what if it is not located on the corner, but it is the next to the one-in-the-corner in the lane, and he has maintained it well. He refused an offer for even $145,000. A year later the market trend changed, and he sold it for $130,000.

Similarly, your friend Ben who wanted to buy a house in a particular location won't pay more than $100,000 because his office friend bought one for $100,000, and that is the fair market value. Ben is willing to forego the offer, even if it is $15,000 higher than his anchored price, and he can afford it. Often when the real estate market is booming, the prices go up, and Ben's of the world either live with a regret or end up paying $10,000 to $15, 000 higher.

It should seem that experts in a subject who have devoted years of their life would not be susceptible to anchoring. For instance, real estate professionals who are in touch with the market and have access to more information seem better placed to not be weighed down by the anchors. But it is not so.

Two business school professors carried out a study with real estate agents in Tucson, Arizona, in U.S. for understanding effect of anchors in real world settings. Two groups of real estate agents were shown one of the two houses, one appraised at $ 74,900 and another at $ 135,000. They also received a 10-page packet containing standard information needed to value the property, including the listed price, apart from walking around the property for twenty minutes. Everything was identical, except the true listed price.

For the house having a true appraised value of $74,900, anchored prices of $65,900 and $ 83,900 were provided to two different groups. For the same house, the appraised values $ 67,811 and $75,190 hovered around the anchored prices.

Average estimates given by real estate agents	
Anchored Listing Price, $	Appraised Value, $
65,900	67,811
83,900	75,190

However, different listed prices for the house having a true appraised value of $ 135,000 were provided to agents as follows:

- listed at 11 to 12 percent below the true appraised value
- 4 percent below appraised value
- 4 percent above the appraised value
- 11 to 12 percent above appraised value

The estimates were as per the table below:

Average estimates given by real estate agents	
Anchored Listing Price, $	Appraised Value, $
119,900	114,204
129,900	126,772
139,900	125,041
149,900	128,754

When asked what were the major considerations in valuing the house, only one in ten mentioned the listing price. By anchoring only one piece of information, the appraisal value could be shifted by thousands of dollars. The powering of anchoring is evident, yet the agents were ignorant of it.

If you feel you are being anchored, then try to reduce the impact or break off the old anchor and establish new one. In case of buying a house, for instance, do the following:

- Consider the opposite, generate reasons and list arguments why the anchor is inappropriate
- Compare the asking price to various criteria: location, neighbourhood, condition of floor, roof, kitchen. Reduce price and adjust accordingly.
- Beforehand, find another property with comparable features, area, and age. This price could be the new anchor.

In a booming real estate market, as a buyer if you are anchored to a low price you may not get the deal as somebody else may pay a higher price. On the other hand, in a weak real estate market, the seller who is asking for a specific price may not be able to sell the property.

Used car salesmen quote a very high initial price much above the fair value, prior to starting negotiations, knowing fully well that the high reference point in the beginning will result in a higher selling price in the end. The mutually agreed amount is always an adjustment from the anchor. Some even focus excessively on one piece of information such as upholstery or stereo or year of manufacture of car. While buying a used car, paying attention to how much mileage the car has already clocked and getting obsessed with odometer reading is a common phenomenon, neglecting other aspects such as condition of tyres, suspension or engine.

In purchasing and selling, either of the parties provides anchors intentionally far from the true value. The problem arises because despite adjustments we tend to remain close to the original anchor. If the anchor were close to the fair value, then there would be no adverse effects.

Anchors of your own making may be difficult to cast off. People who move to a new city find it difficult to shed the old anchored prices of the real estate market. Those who move from an expensive city to a cheaper city rent a pricier house than those who move from a cheaper to an expensive city. Similarly, those shifting to a cheaper city often end up buying a bigger house than required. They are unable to shake off the old anchor. When you move to a new city, it may be a wise idea to rent an accommodation for a while, before buying a house.

Buying the Taj Mahal

Have you visited the Taj Mahal at Agra in India, a stunningly beautiful building? The Nobel Laureate Rabindranath Tagore wrote: It 'rises above the banks of the river like a solitary tear suspended on the cheek of time'.

You stand in a long queue, and mesmerised by the first view, you wish to buy a marble replica of the Taj. A handicrafts seller quotes you $ 500 for the piece you have your eyes on. You bargain hard paying just less than half the price, $240. The initial anchor point of $ 500, though high and absurd makes you feel that you haven't paid more for the Taj Mahal. But in reality if you feel the Taj is worth $240, then only anything downwards of $240 would have been a bargain. So, do remember extreme anchor values induce large anchoring effects. But then you really cannot do much about it, despite knowing you are being misled because you have no way of knowing the fair value.

Tied to a stock

Anchoring is for real and affects everyone, whether knowledgeable or novice. In the stock market, while selling or purchasing further units of the same stock, amateurs and professionals alike get anchored to the price they purchased the stock, ignoring the present actual value and future prospects of the company. Sticking to arbitrary price levels of shares and stock indices without taking into account the latest information is a sure sign of being anchored. A decision in the changed circumstances based on the old information can cost us dear.

People can get anchored to a stock's price without even buying it. When the share price falls, they compare it with the all-time high price and anchored to the peak price rush to buy as it looks cheap.

It is easy to get anchored, but it is difficult to counter it. It's easy to focus on the anchor. In contrast, it is mentally taxing and requires effort to move away from the anchor. Anchors of your mind are like dead-weights, tying you to the ground. Drop the anchor in a different way, by not carrying it with your ship. Let go of all anchors. Let the mind move freely. As the Dutch saying goes: "Better lose the anchor than the whole ship".

Action tips: How to shake off an anchor?

1. **Be aware of the tendency**: The first step is being aware of the tendency to get anchored. Each one of us, whether an expert or an amateur, is liable to fall prey to anchoring. Your mind often falls into this trap while estimating, forecasting, or deciding.

2. **Drop the anchor**: Are you getting obsessed with a particular number, figure, or amount while deciding? Have you created your own anchor? Notice that precise numbers like $197.36 anchor you more. Argue against the anchored number in a deliberate manner, listing reasons the number could be wrong. Drop the anchor.

3. **Delay the final decision**: Don't be in a hurry. Instead, slow down and get extra information, especially when you are buying something, as you might be anchored, totally unaware. Consider the alternatives for negating it and breaking its grip.

4. **Take initiative**: In open negotiations, gain an upper hand by making the first offer. Rather than getting anchored by a price set by somebody else, you anchor the other person by setting a baseline.

5. **Reanchor**: If you are not making the first offer while negotiating, overcome the anchor by reanchoring yourself and establishing a new one.

****

Once you are anchored, it's like tied to an elastic band that keeps pulling you back. You have to keep pushing, despite the elastic band pulling you back, until you snap it

Quick Recap

- Anchoring means while making decisions we rely too much on the first impression, initial idea, specific information, value or number, despite adjusting that value.
- However, none of us can adjust sufficiently to negate the effects of anchor.
- Even an idea, a fact, a number that has no relevance to the situation at hand can anchor us.
- A ridiculously high value can anchor us as much as a plausible value.
- No one is immune to anchoring, be it experts or amateurs. Experts and amateurs are equally susceptible to these effects, irrespective of the field.
- In negotiations, if you do not make the first offer, then overcome anchoring by reanchoring or establishing new anchors.

Rewiring

Refer exercises in the Action Guide under Rewiring: 8. Understanding how you get anchored is important. Even more important is the action you take to negate an anchor and reanchor yourself.

9

Stereotypes and The Law of Small Numbers

"A stereotype may be negative or positive, but even positive stereotypes present two problems: They are clichés, and they present a human being as far more simple and uniform than any human being actually is".

Nancy Kress

The surgeon's dilemma

A father and his son are in a car accident. The father dies at the scene, and the son is rushed to the hospital. At the hospital the surgeon looks at the boy and says, "I can't operate on this boy, he is my son." How can this be? Ponder over it, and read ahead after you have made up your mind or given up. Having a gay dad or a robot as a father is ruled out.

This is an old riddle, also known as the surgeon's dilemma, which shows the inherent unconscious bias in popular imagination that only men could be surgeons. The surgeon is the boy's mother. More than half of us, including those whose mothers are doctors, self-described feminists, belonging to higher income and educational groups, have difficulty in answering this riddle.

Before you think of gender bias, consider the alternative version of the puzzle. A mother and her daughter are in a car accident. The mother is killed on the spot, and her daughter is sent to the hospital. At the hospital, a nurse declines to attend to the patient because "that girl is my daughter". The results were no better. Many could not imagine a male nurse.

We find it difficult to imagine a surgeon mom and a male nurse. A male represents a surgeon and not a nurse, whereas a female represents a nurse and not a surgeon. Such generalizations help us navigate the complex world but do not always reflect our life's experience. Therefore, having a doctor mom does not necessarily mean you will solve the riddle correctly.

In our mind, the stereotype of an average surgeon is of a father. Our judgements are often based on how typical or representative a particular event or happening is of something else. We rely on our memory of a prototype, or average or stereotype. This representativeness is a good mental short cut, a rule of thumb approach that works most of the times, but not always. Though heuristics like this help us in reaching conclusions, fast and quick, they do fail us.

Who is Linda?

Linda is 31 years old, single, outspoken, and very bright. She majored in philosophy. As a student, she was deeply concerned with issues of discrimination and social justice and also participated in anti-nuclear demonstrations.

Based on the above description, rank the following statements about Linda, from most to least likely:

1. Linda is an insurance salesperson.
2. Linda is a bank teller.
3. Linda is a bank teller and is active in the feminist movement.

Most people think option 3, "Linda is a bank teller and is active in the feminist movement" is more likely than option 2, "Linda is a bank teller". And most people are wrong, though fast and quick, as the stereotyped image of what specific characteristics represent a particular person gives an incorrect answer. We commit a mistake known as conjunction fallacy.

Linda is described in a manner resembling our stereotype of a feminist. Probability of a feminist bank teller higher than a bank teller does not make sense. A bank teller is a broader category than the category of feminist bank teller. The latter category, feminist bank teller cannot be more likely than the former, bank teller alone. A sub-set cannot be greater than a set of objects. Even if somebody feels Linda's description does not match that of only a bank teller in option 2, it is still as likely as option 3.

If unrepresentative elements such as a bank teller are combined with representative details, being active in the feminist movement, the description becomes psychologically compelling, goading us in forsaking logic, while making choices. The details render the description riveting, yet these very details preclude us from selecting what is highly likely.

Mental prototypes

Tom is a graduate student in a university with nine fields of specialization:

1. business administration
2. computer science
3. engineering
4. humanities and education
5. law
6. medicine
7. library science
8. physical and life sciences
9. social science and social work

STEREOTYPES AND THE LAW OF SMALL NUMBERS

Here is a brief profile of the student's personality.

Tom is of high intelligence, although lacking in true creativity. He has a need for order and clarity, and for neat and tidy systems in which every detail finds its appropriate place. His writing is rather dull and mechanical, occasionally enlivened by somewhat corny puns and by flashes of imagination of the sci-fi type. He has a strong drive for competence. He seems to feel little sympathy for other people and does not enjoy interacting with others. Self-centered, he nonetheless has a deep moral sense.

Compare your answers to an actual survey done in a university, by dividing the participants in three groups.

In which of these fields is Tom more likely to be a student? How would you rank order these fields in terms of the likelihood that Tom is a student in that field?

The first group which was asked to judge how similar Tom was to the typical graduate student in the nine fields of study ranked as below:

1. computer science
2. engineering
3. business administration
4. physical and life sciences
5. library science
6. law
7. medicine
8. humanities and education
9. social science and social work

A second group was asked to rank on the basis of probability or likelihood of Tom's field. A third group was asked to rank on the basis of relative percentages of graduate students enrolled in these courses at the time.

That the first group, predicted on the basis of similarity conforming to the stereotype of computer science student is not surprising. The second group also gave response similar to the first group. The third group ignored the available statistics that there were far more humanities students than computer science students. This neglect of existing relevant data, the base that indicates probability in absence of any other information leads us to wrong conclusion.

We substitute our stereotypes or representativeness for probability and known chances of an event happening. The three groups, similarity group, probability group, and base rate group reached the same judgement based on mental prototype of an engineering student that matched Tom's description.

Neglecting the existing information or chances of an event in light of new information, without integrating the two is known as the base rate neglect.

Investors in the market often overreact to new event specific information while neglecting the overall context or the base of the information pertaining to a company. For instance, an investor may be overly worry about a company's ability to meet its projected earnings in a particular quarter, disregarding its financial position, growth rates, cash position, and demand for its product among others.

Nobel Prize for ulcers

For decades the doctors believed peptic ulcers in the stomach were caused by stress, spicy food, acid, smoking, and alcohol. In 1983, a 32-year old Australian physician, Professor Barry J. Marshall and Robin Warren after researching concluded that it was not so. Instead they discovered the culprit was a bacterium, Helicobacter pylori, causing gastritis, ulcers, and stomach cancer. Therefore, this could be cured by simple antibiotics. But nobody believed them.

STEREOTYPES AND THE LAW OF SMALL NUMBERS

Around 800,000 people die from related stomach cancer each year. On the one hand, the patients were dying of bleeding ulcers, on the other hand, the reputed medical journals would not even publish their findings. For the medical community, the proposition germ causes ulcers was akin to saying the earth is flat. In fact, the director of the Vanderbilt University School of Medicine ridiculed the finding as "the most preposterous thing I'd ever heard".

Frustrated with stonewalling and scepticism of the scientific community, in 1984 Marshall drank a cloudy broth containing the bacteria to test it on himself and prove his findings. Marshall developed gastritis and the lab tests confirmed he had been infected with the bacterium. He cured himself with antibiotics. In the end the saga had a happy ending. He and Warren were awarded the Nobel Prize for Medicine in 2005.

What caused the scientific community to ignore the evidence put forth by Marshall and Warren is the general assumption that the symptoms of a disease should resemble either its cause or its cure or both. Treatment has to be representative of the illness. Like should go with like.

Similarly, doctors and laypersons alike found it difficult to believe that malaria was transmitted from person to person by particular species of mosquitoes and not through bad air as was thought since the time of Romans. A tiny mosquito, the cause of malaria, could not be representative of a fatal disease, malaria.

In real world, stereotyping clouds our judgement and often can be the difference between a prison sentence or not found guilty, even going to the gallows. Does an accuse fit the stereotype of what a criminal looks, an image formed over the years from watching movies, reading novels, watching television or simply observing people. If yes, the jury members are more likely to declare the accused as guilty. Also, does the jury view the crime defendant is accused of as falling into a category as heinous, for example, raping a child versus an adult or abducting a child versus an adult.

We also tend to be disappointed when individuals in certain roles and professions do not conform to our representative image. In fact, recall the number of times you have read magazines describing somebody as "45-year old Jim is the last person anybody would mistake for a computer science professor. At 6'4" he looks more like a bouncer at a local bar". After all, computer science professors are supposed to be nerdy, intelligent, and weak, not muscular. A farmer is supposed to look the part, hard-working and tough. Again, a librarian fits the stereotype of someone who is shy, helpful, tidy, and orderly.

People genuinely remember seeing behaviour that is expected, further reinforcing stereotypes. We all believe in stereotypes based on socio-economic status, colour of the skin, race, nationality, educational qualifications, profession, geography, and culture.

I-know-a-man syndrome

You know your uncle smoked two pack of cigarettes a day and lived to the ripe old age of 90. Therefore, smoking does not kill, and you can smoke to your heart's content. Your conclusion is absolutely wrong, arrived by taking one example and generalizing it.

I know a man who jumped from sixth floor of a building and survived. But it would not be safe for all of us to do so. It's an exception. We all know of one such instance in life and work. Let an exception not become the rule for your decisions.

You decide to sell you old car and are looking to buy a new reliable small car. You have read all the surveys, watched the videos, and soaked information from various internet forums. You have narrowed down to either a Volkswagen or a Ford. You talked to a few Ford and Volkswagen owners, and finally the majority suggests that Volkswagen is more reliable and easy to maintain. Suddenly, you remember your old uncle who had a Volkswagen, until two years ago. You talk to him over the phone. He says buy anything, but never ever buy Volkswagen, narrating his woes due to frequent breakdowns. He advises you to buy a Ford.

Like most people you may be tempted to listen to your uncle who has always given you right advice, and that is why you trust him, placing less emphasis on, if not ignoring the consumer reports and the experts' opinion.

Don't follow the law of small numbers

Well, you are not the one to indulge in hasty generalisations, and you take pride in the fact that you take rational decisions by researching carefully. Be careful to check if you are not following the law of small numbers. Basing your conclusions on talking to a small number of people or happenings or small data set or sample size can lead you to take extreme positions and wrong decisions.

Let us say we decide to select randomly only five people to represent the United States of America or the United Kingdom. Will only five whites or African-Americans or Hispanic or Indians or Chinese or a combination of these can correctly represent the population of the U.S. Just as one person does not represent the entire population, so too a small group does not.

We would be amiss to conclude a mutual fund manager is a stellar performer because the fund he manages has provided above market average returns in the last three years. It would be wise to assess his returns over a longer period of time. What does a 10-year record look like? Are the preceding three-year returns an extreme number, skewing the judgement?

In activities where random events or luck plays an important role, we would be unwise to base our conclusions on the basis of a small number of observations. Otherwise extreme outcomes, high or low, found in small sample sizes and time periods will fool us. We will find a relationship where it does not exist or miss where it exists. Random numbers, though less can generate patterns.

That is why when you took a walk in the casino in Chapter 1, you saw patterns in the last five numbers where the ball landed on the roulette wheel. But you could never be sure about it.

Though not all marketers are liars, now you know enough not to believe commercials stating four out of five housewives recommend this refrigerator. Instead of unconsciously following the law of small numbers, what we need to follow is the law of large numbers, that is, when we increase a sample size, it becomes truly representative of the entire set of observations.

Mozart effect

In 1993, psychologist Frances Rauscher and two other researchers carried out an experiment and published their findings in the journal Nature. They claimed that after listening to Mozart's 1781 sonata for two pianos (K448) for 10 minutes, students enhanced their cognitive abilities. The study included only 79 undergraduate students out of which 36 students scored 8 to 9 points higher on the spatial IQ reasoning subtest.

The study based on outcome of only 36 students generated lot of publicity, excitement and was interpreted by popular media as if Mozart's music can enhance general intelligence or IQ. The New York Times wrote that listening to Mozart could improve performance in the SAT. In follow up books and articles, many claimed classical music could benefit mental faculties of infants. It could transform health, education, and well-being. A panacea had been found.

A few years later in 1998, the governor of Georgia even issued a bill that the state would provide every child born in Georgia with a free tape or CD of classical music. He made legislators listen some of Beethoven's "Ode to Joy" played on a tape recorder and asked "Now, don't you feel smarter already? Not to be left behind in producing smarter children, Florida passed a law, mandating state-funded day-care centers to play at least one hour of classical music every day.

These results have never been replicated in any of the subsequent studies so far. A "Mozart effect", as suggested by Rauscher has not been confirmed. It is a legend now relegated to the popular myths of psychology. The original study may have shown the effect as claimed, but the size of the study was too small, only 36. The law of small numbers prevails.

A person is loving and caring especially toward the children. You are asked to guess the person's gender, a man or a woman. What is your quick and fast answer? And what's the slow and reflective one?

Easy availability, fast action

Humans also have a tendency to believe what comes to their mind first represents something. This, however, is not the case. Though relying on what is easily available enables quick judgement and avoids effort involved in critical thinking and analysis.

While evaluating any topic or subject, the mind operates under the implicit belief that what has been recalled first is important. And it also believes what is retrieved easily will have a higher likelihood of occurring again. But the mind recalls easily what has happened recently, made the most impression on it or what it observes itself.

People saw aeroplanes crashing into twin towers on 9/11 on television and the repeated media coverage made such a vivid impact that they concluded air travel was the most dangerous form of air travel, forsaking it for quite some time. In reality, a person is more likely to die in a road accident than in an airplane crash. Substituting road travel for air travel for covering long distances and travelling thousands of miles as such would increase the odds of having a road accident. Similarly, after a major train crash, people choose to travel by car instead of by rail in a mistaken belief that they were travelling safely.

Similarly, after the Italian cruise ship Costa Concordia struck an underwater rock, would you have concluded that holidaying on a cruise ship is dangerous? Just because something has happened recently or more frequently, it does not mean it will happen again. Similarly, if something has occurred on a large scale, it does not imply it will again happen on a similar magnitude. Imagine people dismissing the real risks and worrying about the wrong risk of dying in an air crash.

Talking of car accidents, if two of your acquaintances are involved in a road accident, you may be convinced about roads becoming less safe, and you yourself may meet with an accident. If you have been involved in one you may believe that meeting with another car accident is highly likely, though the base rates are much different. After a natural disaster like a hurricane, people are more likely to buy an insurance for hurricane than before.

Supervisors appraising their employee's performance will recall instances of good or bad behaviour which appear to be more than others. They also give more weight to the recent performance in the two or three months preceding the evaluation than the previous nine months, as these can be recalled without much effort.

Going by media reports, some people may be scared of falling prey to violent crime. The media coverage for people who are murdered is higher than those with stomach cancer, leading to easy recall of murder. In reality, chances of dying due to stomach cancer are five times more frequent than due to murder, but people think murder is 1.6 times more frequent than stomach cancer.

Lottery organisers never advertise stating your real chances of winning vary from one in a 13 million to 32 million, depending upon the lottery. If they were to do so, none of us would never buy a ticket. Yet, so many lotteries are being run profitably, signifying no dearth of ticket buyers. Instead, what they do is promote the jackpot winners, barraging all of us continuously through media. People judge their own chances by easy recall of winners, magnifying their own likelihood of winning. When recent winners come to mind, we are more likely to buy a ticket than while thinking about the losers.

Chances of getting struck by lightning, killed by a shark, or hit by a meteor are much higher than winning the jackpot in the Powerball lottery. But somebody has to win it, and why can't it be you. Promotional phrases for the lottery or a lucky draw, "it could be you", carrying a lot of promise are technically true, but rarely turn out to be true.

Action tips: How to keep off the trap of stereotyping and available information?

1. **Do not generalize**: Generalizing leads to stereotyping of people, events, or groups. Stereotypes are not always correct.

2. **New information**: Do not lay more emphasis on new information, neglecting the existing information. Combine the base rate, prevailing information with the new one.

3. **Easy recall**: Things that have happened recently may not happen again. Do not base your decisions on the easily recalled information that may be insufficient. Think and recall not so memorable events: how many people haven't won the lottery; how many haven't met with an accident on the road you travel.

4. **Small numbers**: Decisions are likely to be wrong, when based on personal anecdotal experience from somebody whom you know closely or a small number of happenings or sample size.

5. **Availability versus relevance**: Please know if the information is truly relevant, or are you laying emphasis on it just because of its easy availability. Do not take a shortcut.

6. **Check the key decision making piece**: Is your decision influenced by an important piece of information? If it is so, whether it is really important, representing something or it simply reflects recent or otherwise memorable experiences.

Quick Recap

Stereotyping

- Stereotyping is a mental shortcut to make quick judgements and decisions, by simplifying complexity but at the risk of going wrong.
- We select information that represents details of our stereotypes and disregard information that does not conform to our stereotypes.
- We decide the likelihood of an event by comparing it to an existing stereotype in our mind. We tend to ignore prevailing chances in favour of interesting information about an individual case that is easily available and recalled.
- We think that events that happened recently are more likely to happen again.

Law of small numbers

- We often follow the "law of small numbers", i.e., take decisions by talking to a single person or on the basis of a small sample size and, hence, likely to go wrong.

Rewiring

Refer exercises in the Action Guide under Rewiring: 9. Understanding the power of stereotyping and the hazard of predicting an event on the basis of few earlier occurrences should fool proof you against these mental traps.

10

Memories Are Not Forever

"The difference between false memories and true ones is the same as for jewels: It is always the false ones that look the most real, the most brilliant".

Salvador Dali

Your mind nags you

Bluma Zeigarnik was sitting in a restaurant in Vienna in the 1920s, along with her colleagues. When she ordered lunch, the waiter did not write anything down but remembered exactly who had ordered what. The Soviet psychologist was impressed by the waiter's ability. After sometime she went back to the restaurant to collect her jacket, which she had left there.

To her utter surprise the waiter, who had a superhuman memory, did not recognize her. Intrigued by his behavior, she questioned the waiter who, in turn, explained it was normal behavior on part of all waiters in the restaurant. They could remember orders placed by the customers without any great effort and match these with the diners at the tables. As soon as the order was served and the moment diners left the restaurant after making payment, it was as if the memories of these orders disappeared. The waiters simply forgot about them and focused on the next set of diners.

Bluma conducted further experiments and concluded we remember unfinished tasks better than finished tasks. Incomplete tasks hold tremendous power over us as they occupy our short-term memory until we complete them. While holding tasks in short-term memory, rehearsing them is necessary or else they disappear. It is like juggling balls in the air, and you can't juggle too many at one time.

Whether important or unimportant, unfinished tasks will haunt you and distract you. Start too many tasks, leave them open, and rest assured your stress will increase. If too many important tasks are left incomplete, it may lead to anxiety and take an emotional toll as well. On the other hand, completing such tasks gives us a sense of accomplishment and increases our well-being.

The power of our mind to nag us over unfinished tasks can be utilized to our advantage. To overcome procrastination, life coaches and personal development experts often exhort us to start a task, taking that first step, no matter how small. The easier the first step is the better it is. Once you start, the incomplete task acts as its own reminder.

Students find it useful to break up their study sessions rather than cram everything in one sitting. While taking a break, when they focus on something else, the intrusive thoughts about the information will enable better consolidation of information and recall. Ongoing thinking during interruptions keeps the information in mind.

If we start a task and leave it unfinished, it will keep on intruding on our thoughts. Thereafter, we are at the mercy of our brains. We would rather be careful to start a new task. Alas, there is a way to let our brain stop thinking about the pending task. Write the tasks in a manner that convinces your brain you will tackle it. Your brain cannot notice the difference between a task that you actually complete and the one which you defer by making a note. Productivity experts always tell you to have a reliable system whereby you note down all the tasks, freeing your short-term memory. Once you develop trust in your system, you can focus on the task at hand, one at a time, without being bothered about the pending ones.

Those looking for creative ideas and solutions put this trait of human mind to even better use. They pose questions, seed a thought, and then let go of it. The mind dwells on it, making connections, as they engage in some other activity, springing solutions when least expected, in shower, while walking, or doing nothing.

The absurd and the isolated

Go through the following two lists consisting of 10 items each.

LIST 1	LIST 2
9	TOZ
12	DUQ
3	HOL
16	COS
QXK	QXK
5	DRF
14	TXP
11	XMS
2	FTH
7	HZL

Unless you are a memory champion or have not used any memory technique, what are you likely to remember. The syllable QXK in list 1 must have caught your eye as it sticks out. Whereas, if you went through list 2 first, it is highly unlikely that you would remember the syllable QXK. We remember an isolated item from the list of similar items compared to a list where all the items are similar, though their position in the list may be same.

Students highlight important portions in the textbooks for making it stand out in their mind and memorizing better. In a text document, we can highlight, make letters bold, render it in italic, or underline among others. A green apple in a bunch of red apples will catch you eye. Companies highlight certain features of their products to stand out from the crowd and get their customers' attention. In the above list, if one of the syllables was in red it would catch your attention.

LIST 1	LIST 2
9	TOZ
12	DUQ
3	HOL
16	COS
QXK	QXK
5	DRF
14	TXP
11	XMS
2	FTH
7	HZL

The unusual, unconventional, and unexpected is always more memorable than the mundane. In fact, memory champions turn mundane facts, figures, and numbers into the absurd to remember them. Consider the list of items: Elephant, bottle, car, shoes, necklace and pizza. If you have to remember the list, you would do well to turn it into an absurd sequence of events and visualize it. Picture an elephant on a busy road wearing pink shoes and a diamond necklace, eating a domino's pizza, drinking water from the bottle, and spraying it over a passing car.

Similarly, if you are told not to think about a pink elephant, you would definitely think about it. We all never forget things that stand out from the rest. Surprises grab our attention. As the old journalistic adage goes: "If a man bites a dog it's news, if a dog bites a man it isn't."

But a flip side exists to this habit of our mind. When our attention is consumed by something different, then as a result, we pay less attention towards the rest and remember it less. You need to be aware of where your mind is being directed.

All memory is false memory

Error in memory is often the norm, not the exception. It is not only those with a debilitating disease like Alzheimer's but perfectly healthy individuals suffer from false memories. These are memories based on not any real occurrences but have real consequences like joy, happiness, sadness, anxiety and trauma.

'I remember being born' shows 692 million searches in Google search engine. We know that nobody can remember events of their infancy, as babies cannot form and store long-term memories. Yet people claim to remember the hospital room they were born, the color of the crib, and how warm they felt inside their mother's womb. It is only from around two years of age we form memories lasting into our adulthood. Before that age, everything is a novelty, and children do not even know what is important, what needs to be remembered. Nor do we have the ability to process such happenings. Young children do have memories but not the ones that last until adulthood.

Once it gets a grip over you, there is no way to distinguish a false memory from a true memory.

Nostalgia

Nostalgia is longing for our past, about memories of our good old days, though those days may not have been that good. Generally, it is about our memories between 10 to 30 years of age, as we retain the most memories of our teens and twenties. These are most emotional and, therefore, vivid, most significant and most unexpected events in our life. When we are nostalgic we do not recall what actually happened, but we feel good by validating our past, our thoughts and actions, reliving the good times.

While personal nostalgia is common in face of uncertainty, unhappiness, or instability, in times of transition, we are also faced with historical nostalgia. While meeting the challenges of modern life, surrounded by technological advances, social and political changes, polarized atmosphere, breakdown of community increases the yearning for a bygone era, the romanticized distant past when troubles were few and life was simple.

Our ability to perceive the world is imperfect and limited. The misperceptions of our reality are parked in our memories that we recall later. We believe pseudo memories as real and mistake imagined events for reality.

Most eyewitness accounts are wrong

Apart from a confidently held memory, should not a memory in great detail inspire confidence in its veracity. No. Just because someone speaks with confidence, emotion, and paints a rich picture of an event does not mean it happened.

False memories have often tricked not only those who recall events but also lawyers and judges. Eyewitness to crimes—murder, rape or robbery—are often unable to give an accurate account of the happenings, despite their best intentions. Memory does not record exact details like a video camera; instead, it records only the gist of the events.

In June 1995, Joseph Abbitt was sentenced to 110 years in prison in addition to two consecutive life sentences on two counts of first degree rape, one count of first degree burglary, and two counts of first degree kidnapping. The crime: in North Carolina, in May 1991, he broke into a home through a kitchen window in the early morning and raped two teenage sisters, who were getting ready for school, at knife point.

Although the victims did not see the attacker's face clearly, they told investigators that their attacker looked like Joseph Abbitt, an African American. He had previously lived in the neighborhood and had visited their home. Moreover, the sisters separately identified him in a photo lineup. Four years after the crime, the sisters testified before a jury in June 1995 that he was the person who had attacked them. No wonder, the jury convicted Abbitt of rape, burglary, and kidnapping, pronouncing a harsh sentence.

In 2005, the North Carolina Center on Actual Innocence for assistance accepted his case for assistance. DNA testing proved his innocence beyond doubt, and he was set free in 2009. He was wrongly convicted and served 14 years for heinous crimes he had not committed.

In the United States alone, between 1989 to 2019, out of hundreds and thousands convicted of serious crimes, 367 people have been exonerated by DNA testing. The Innocence Project in the United States estimates that more than 75 % of cases wrongful conviction are due to false eyewitness identification.

Mistaken identity is a common phenomenon, but members of the jury give weight to the eyewitness accounts, amplified by the degree of confidence. The victim often becomes more confident about an erroneous memory, by repeated recalling of the event in a certain way. In fact, false memories can trick all of us, the lawyers, juries and the eyewitnesses as well.

A victim may not be able to recall accurate details of events due to stress. However, where the eyewitnesses are not victims, they may fill in the gaps due to fading of memory or offer information about which they are unsure, though with good intentions to solve the case. Frequent errors arise while constructing a memory. The eyewitnesses, for instance, without being aware often include inexact information after an event.

How you enquire about an event, and the kind of questions you ask about the memory of an event matters a lot, failing which you may head in a different direction altogether. Whether it's a bystander who witnessed a crime or your college roommate who parties hard, do not ask close ended and leading questions. Asking questions about the color of his eyes or was he an African- American will lead to wrong answers. It is better to let the person tell his own account, without interrupting and prompting. Resist the urge to ask too many questions, and if you have to limit yourself to asking open ended questions, ask for example, can you tell us a bit more about this?

It is not only individuals who remember events that never actually occurred or recall events differently from the way they happened. Groups have a propensity to do so as even collective memories get distorted. You have a memory that you trust to be true, and others also confirm it to be true; however, in reality it may be false. For instance, take the 'Mandela effect'. A false memory perpetuates that the great South African leader, revolutionary, and Nobel Prize winner Nelson Mandela died in the 1980s in a prison. He actually breathed his last on 5 December 2013. In fact, he was awarded the Nobel peace prize in 1993 and served as President of South Africa from 1994 to 1999.

In such cases, you may need to verify separately, if the memory is authentic.

Editing the past

The idea that our memory is perfect is a big myth. It is not a video camera that can replay events of our childhood or a fortnight ago. It is built to change, not recall facts; it is designed to make good decisions in the moment. In fact, we edit our past with present experiences, new happenings. Our mind, our memory to be specific, rewrites, overwrites, reframes the past events to create a story to fit our current world, making it more relevant and useful for now. The hippocampus in our brain acts like a film editor, adding special effects.

That is why your most cherished memories may not be true and perfectly accurate in any case. Whenever we bring back an old memory, we face the risk of changing it, knowingly or unknowingly. Just as when you open a word document on your laptop, you can edit or delete it, so too when you remember something you can erase it or manipulate it. You do not write your memories once but every time you recall them, the critical window for rewriting or reconsolidation being small.

Action tips: How to prevent the pitfalls of memory?

1. **Prevent mind nagging**: Don't have too many unfinished tasks at any given time as they increase stress. If required, note your pending tasks in a reliable system where you can refer back.

2. **Seeing in isolation**: Beware if you are seeing something in isolation, and it seems to stick in your memory.

3. **Beware of nostalgia**: It is the feeling for the good old days when everything was fine. In a state of nostalgia, you do not recall what actually happened, but what you believe happened.

4. **Eyewitness accounts**: Just because you were eyewitness to a happening does not mean you will recall it correctly. Even if somebody recalls an incident in great detail accompanied by emotion, it doesn't mean it happened. False memories can trick us.

5. **False memories**: Claiming to remember things that are impossible is a common occurrence. These memories feel real but are not based on actual experience.

6. **Rewrite your past**: Turn the feature of false memory to your advantage, by updating itself as desired. Choose negative events from your past, imagine them, and bring to a happy ending. Use imagery, and rescript your past memories.

Quick Recap

- We remember incomplete tasks better than those are completed. However, they occupy our short-term memory. Too many incomplete tasks create stress.
- If we see something that stands out in isolation, we are more likely to remember it.
- We can lay too much emphasis on events in our past due to nostalgia and draw wrong conclusions. Nostalgia is a distortion of long-term memory.
- Human memory is fallible and not accurate. It is pliable and malleable as the information changes over time. False memories feel real but are not based on actual experience.
- There is no way to tell apart a false memory from a true one once it takes hold on you. Vivid memories with conviction can be totally false.

Rewiring

Refer exercises in the Action Guide under Rewiring: 10. You should be able to understand that our memories get distorted, and false memories can take hold over us. Even eyewitness accounts cannot be entirely accurate.

Annexure: Solution to card selection problem in Chapter 4

The rule was "If the card shows an even number on one face, then its opposite face is red". Only a card with both an even number on one face and something other than red on the other face can invalidate this rule:

- If the 3 card is red (or brown), that doesn't violate the rule. The rule makes no claims about odd numbers.
- If the 8 card is not red, it violates the rule.
- If the red card is odd (or even), that doesn't violate the rule. The red color is not exclusive to even numbers.
- If the brown card is even, it violates the rule

Therefore, the 8 card and the brown card is the right answer.

(Reference: Wikipedia)

Author Bio

Andrew is a former Air force officer and a strategist. Believing that it is people who make teams, groups, and organizations, he focuses on individuals with strategies for increasing productivity, improving performance, and overcoming diverse challenges in life.

He has survived an earthquake, numerous ski falls, and a hang gliding mishap. A lifelong learner, his varied experience informs his world view and writing.

Notes and References

1. The Arden Dictionary of Shakespeare Quotations, Jane Armstrong
2. The Oxford Dictionary of Modern Quotations, Elizabeth Knowles
3. The Basic Laws of Human Stupidity, Carlo M. Cippola
4. The Seven Sins of Memory: How the Mind Forgets and Remembers, Daniel Schacter
5. The Memory Illusion: Remebering, Forgetting and the Science of False Memory, Julia Shaw
6. Great Myths of Psychology, Lillienfield, Lynn, Ruscio
7. The Optimism Bias; A Tour of the Irrationally Positive Brain, Tali Sharot
8. Why Smart People Make Big Money Mistakes - And How to Correct Them: Lessons from the New Science of Behavioral Economics, Gary Belsky, Simon & Schuster, 2000
9. Behavioural Investing: A Practitioners Guide to Applying Behavioural Finance, Wiley, 2002
10. Behavioral Finance: Understanding the Social, Cognitive, and Economic Debates, Burton, Edwin, Shah, Sunit N
11. The Psychology of Investing, Nofsinger
12. The Illusion of Risk Control. What Does it Take to Live With Uncertainty? Motet, Gilles, Bieder
13. Mental Models and the Mind: Current developments in Cognitive Psychology, Neuroscience and Philosophy of Mind: 138, Carsten, Gottfried
14. Self-insight: Roadblocks and Detours On the Path to Knowing Thyself, David Dunning
15. Overconfidence and War: The Havoc and Glory of Positive Illusions, Dominic D.P. Johnson, Harvard University Press
16. Failing to Win: Perceptions of Victory and Defeat in International Politics, Dominic D.P. Johnson and Dominic Tierney, Harvard University Press
17. How We Reason, Philip Johnson Laird, Oxford University Press
18. The Neuroscience of Emotion, Ralph Andolphs, David Anderson
19. Thinking, Fast and Slow, Daniel Kahneman, Penguin Books Ltd
20. Cognitive Illusions: Intriguing phenomena in thinking, judgment and memory, Rüdiger F. Pohl, Routledge
21. A model of heuristic judgment, Daniel Kahneman1 and Shane Frederick,Levin, Schneider and Gaeth
22. Anomalies: The Endowment Effect, Loss Aversion, and Status Quo Bias, Kahneman, Knetsch, Thaler
23. Blind or Biased? Justitia's Susceptibility to Anchoring Effects in the Courtroom Based on Given Numerical Representations, Birte Englich
24. Responses to Katie Overy's Paper, "Can Music Really 'Improve' the Mind?" (Psychology of Music, 26, 97-99)
25. Cheating and Loss Aversion: Do People Lie More to Avoid a Loss? Grolleau, Kocher, Sutan
26. Cognitive Biases in Military Decision Making, Lieutenant Colonel Michael J. Janser United States Army
27. Confirmation Bias: A Ubiquitous Phenomenon in Many Guises, Raymond S. Nickerson
28. Do Digger Wasps Commit the Concorde Fallacy? , Dawkins & Brockmann
29. The Framing of Decisions and the Psychology of Choice, Tversky and Kahneman
30. Gambling with the House Money and Trying to Break Even: The Effects of Prior Outcomes on Risky Choice, Thaler and Johnson
31. Searching for Explanations: How the Internet Inflates Estimates of Internal Knowledge, Fisher, Goddu & Keil
32. Lessons from Everest: The Interaction of Cognitive Bias, Psychological Safety, and System Complexity, Michael A. Roberto, California Management Review
33. Like goes with like: The role of representativeness in erroneous and pseudo-scientific beliefs, Gilovich and Savitsky
34. The better-than-my-average effect: The relative impact of peak and average performances in assessments of the self and others, Williams and Gilovich, Journal of Experimental Social Psychology

35. Helicobacter Connections, Nobel Lecture, December 8, 2005 by Barry J. Marshall
36. Waiting game, By Frank Partnoy, Financial Times, June 22, 2012
37. Playing Dice With Criminal Sentences: The Influence of
38. Irrelevant Anchors on Experts' Judicial Decision Making, Englich, Mussweiler, and Strack
39. Behind bars but above the bar: Prisoners consider themselves more prosocial than non-prisoners, Constantine Sedikides, Rosie Meek, Mark D. Alicke and Sarah Taylor, British Journal of Social Psychology
40. Music and Spatial Task Performance: A Causal Relationship, Rauscher, Shaw, et al, University of California
41. Experts, Amateurs, and Real Estate: An Anchoring-and- Adjustment Perspective on Property Pricing Decisions, Northcraft and Neale
42. Conviction of the Innocent: Lessons from Psychological Research, Tunnel Vision, Keith A. Findley, University of Wisconsin Law School
43. The Mozart Effect: Music Listening is Not Music Instruction, Rauscher and Hinton
44. The "Saw-It-All-Along" Effect: Demonstrations of Visual Hindsight Bias, Harley, Loftus

9 798855 306048